365
Ways to Drive
a Liberal
CRAZY

365
Ways to Drive
a Liberal
Crazy

...

James Delingpole

Since 1947
REGNERY
PUBLISHING, INC.
An Eagle Publishing Company • Washington, DC

Library of Congress Cataloging-in-Publication Data

Delingpole, James, 1965-
 365 ways to drive a liberal crazy / by James Delingpole.
     p. cm.
 ISBN 978-1-59698-642-8
 1. Liberalism—United States—Humor. 2. United States—Politics and government--Humor. I. Title.
 PN6231.L47D45 2010
 320.51'30973--dc22

                         2010036061

Published in the United States by
Regnery Publishing, Inc.
One Massachusetts Avenue, NW
Washington, DC 20001
www.regnery.com

Manufactured in the United States of America
10 9 8 7 6 5 4 3 2 1

Books are available in quantity for promotional or premium use. Write to Director of Special Sales, Regnery Publishing, Inc., One Massachusetts Avenue NW, Washington, DC 20001, for information on discounts and terms or call (202) 216-0600.

Distributed to the trade by:
Perseus Distribution
387 Park Avenue South
New York, NY 10016

Why Annoying Liberals Is Easy, Fun, and Necessary

It's pretty simple, actually: the facts of life are conservative. You know that, I know that. Unfortunately the half of the human species that *doesn't* know is right now ruining the country.

America: we have a problem! What in tarnation are we going to do?

Well, first the bad news. Assassination is right out. Not only is it illegal but it also runs the extreme risk of granting the victim a JFK halo. Can you imagine that? The "Porkulus" package, the Cairo speech, Obamacare, the failure to address illegal immigration, and the ongoing socialistic destruction of the economy all suddenly being hailed by posterity as just the first bold, noble, brilliant moves of a presidency so great it made Camelot look like the dog days of Jimmy Carter? Why, even to think of such a horror is almost as bad as trying to imagine Al Gore's sweating, blubbery, alleged advances on that hapless Portland massage therapist. Almost.

Now the good news. Who needs assassination when you can inflict death by a thousand cuts instead?

And who is going to administer that death by a thousand cuts? Why YOU are, of course!

You may not be able to make your displeasure known personally to Obama, Biden, Reid, Pelosi, Schumer, Gore, or any of the rest of that ragbag of socialists, crypto-communists, agitators, eco-fascists, rabble-rousers, and malcontents associated with this dismal and disastrous administration. But you can certainly do the next best thing.

Make this day and every day an annoy-the-hell-out-of-a-liberal day.

Not only is baiting liberals tremendously good sport, but it requires remarkably little effort.

Liberals are easy meat for conservatives for several good reasons.

1. Liberals have no sense of humor.
2. Liberals have no facts on their side.
3. Liberals are hypocrites.
4. God, being conservative Himself, hates liberalism at least as much as you do, which is why He created reasons 1, 2, and 3.

In this book we offer 365 suggestions as to how you might go about annoying liberals. The list is not exhaustive, but with luck it will offer you a few pointers on some of the most satisfying and effective liberal-baiting techniques.

They range from jokes (liberals hate jokes) to clever quotes (some of which illustrate why conservatism is the only political philosophy that works, others which illustrate why liberalism is so foolish). They include facts to deploy against liberals in an argument (remember: facts to a liberal are as garlic to a vampire) and techniques to counter the devious tricks liberals so often deploy in debate (to make up for the fact that they have no facts). They include glorious, scurrilous rumors to spread about well-known liberals which, even though probably not true, darn well ought to be. They include references to movies (which liberals like to think of as purely liberal things) and rock (which liberals also like to think of as a purely liberal thing), both of which we hereby reclaim for the cause of conservatism. And they include various facts from history which show that everything that was ever good and true and right is, was, and always shall be conservative, and everything that was ever bad, mendacious, and wrong inevitably began/begins with "l" and ends "-iberal."

Clear enough for you? Good. So what are you waiting for?

Set to work. Start driving those liberals crazy.

**Every day is a good day
to annoy a liberal.
Don't put it off till tomorrow—
get started today!**

Write out on index cards, "I will annoy liberals every day."

Then put them in prominent places in your home, your car, and your office.

Tell a joke:

Q: Why was Obama so disappointed when he went to a screening of *The Men Who Stare at Goats*?

A: Being a Muslim, he thought there would be more romance.

Prefer "chairman" to "chair," "chairperson," or "chairwoman"; "fireman" to "firefighter"; etc.

Conservative women are quite robust and sensible enough not to worry about PC nonsense like our language's in-built "phallocentrism." However, when trying to give offense, "actress" is perfectly acceptable since liberal actresses who take themselves seriously much prefer the term "actor."

If it's cold outside, deploy Global Warming Fun.

· ·

NO. 1.

Say to every liberal you meet, at every opportunity: "Brrr, it's cold. Makes you think we could do with a bit more *global warming*." Dig them hard in the ribs to emphasize how funny your joke is. Otherwise, there's a danger they might not get it. They're weird that way, liberals.

Pop 'round to your nearest extremist mosque with a bottle of Pepsi. Say to the Imam:

"Look I know you guys say you love death more than you love this stuff. But have a sip—you might just change your mind."

6

Deploy the *Reductio ad Hitleram.*

NO. 1.

In the conservative arsenal against liberal smugness, compla-cency, and general disgustingness, this is the equivalent of the daisy cutter bomb: devastating and unanswerable because it's true. Hitler was a National *Socialist*. This means liberals, who are socialists in all but name, are Nazis. Should they question this—as they will—refer them to Jonah Goldberg's indispensible *Liberal Fascism*, in which all is explained: the red in the Nazi flag represents communism; the person largely responsible for the common miscon-ception that Nazism was a movement of the political right was Joseph Stalin—who wanted to hide the embarrassing truth of just how close it was to Soviet communism; the Nazis were no bigger on free enterprise and liberty than the Obama administration is.

Tell a joke:

Q: How can you tell when a liberal politician is lying?

A: His lips move.

8

Start a rumor:

Ingrid Newkirk, founder of the animal rights extremist group PETA, wasn't just blowing off empty rhetoric when she said, "When it comes to feelings, a rat is a dog is a pig is a boy…" Her eco-friendly home is powered entirely by her "family" of adopted pigmy children whom she has rescued from the war-torn Congo. In return for her generous hospitality, each child spends no more than five hours a day in her basement "fun-running" on the giant hamster-style wheel that powers her turbine generator. It used to be eight hours, but she found that on a compulsory vegetarian diet the kids tended to flake out from exhaustion.

Join a liberal reading group.

Propose as your first book choice *The Bell Curve* by Richard J. Herrnstein and Charles Murray.

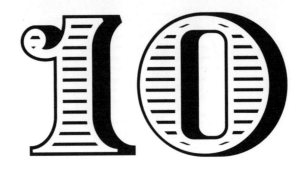

Quote G. Gordon Liddy:

"A liberal is someone who feels a great debt to his fellow man, which debt he proposes to pay off with your money."

Always refer, in pitying, sympathetic tones,

to the "Liberal psychopathology." This implies that liberalism is a form of mental illness. Which it is.

12

Give them another reason why President Obama has GOT to go.

. . . .

NO. 1.

He has the reverse Midas touch. Almost everything he touches turns to You Know What: when he flew to Copenhagen to plead Chicago's case for the 2016 Olympics, the International Olympic Committee gave them to Rio instead; when he flew to Copenhagen again for the global warming summit, Air Force One was engulfed by a blizzard on landing and the conference ended in failure; when he campaigned in Massachusetts to save "Ted Kennedy's seat" the unthinkable happened: the liberal Democrat lost. You get the idea.

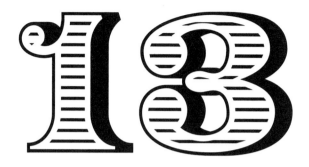

13

Tell them the Bono joke.

Bono is at a U2 concert and asks the crowd for some quiet. Slowly, to rapt silence from the audience, he begins clapping his hands and says into the microphone: "Every time I clap my hands a child in Africa dies." A voice from near the front of the audience pipes up: "Well, stop clapping then."

14

Watch a TV show/movie with a liberal and spend the entire time deconstructing the PC subtext of the casting.

"Well that guy clearly didn't commit the crime. We're only meant to think he did because he's black. But later on our prejudices will be challenged by the revelation that, guess what, the guy who really did it was the nice-seeming, middle class, white, Christian businessman."

Refer to the "Fairness Doctrine" as the "Unfairness Doctrine."

The liberals have captured Google, Wikipedia, most of the print media, television, and Hollywood. In what way is it "fair" to give them an "equal say" in talk radio as well? Liberal talk radio doesn't get "equal" ratings; the unfairness doctrine is really just another socialist effort kill another industry (by making talk radio boring and "forcing" government to take it over).

On his birthday (January 17), quote Benjamin Franklin:

"They that can give up essential liberty to obtain a little temporary safety, deserve neither liberty nor safety." Tell your liberal friends Franklin was referring to government-controlled health care.

Quote with appropriate reverence and non-judgmental, multicultural appreciation the great Iranian religious leader Ayatollah Khomeini:

. . . .

To marry a girl before she begins menstruating is "a divine blessing." If your liberal friend starts sputtering, cheerfully inquire, "Who are you to judge another culture—you're not Islamophobic, are you?"

18

Start a rumor:

Treasury Secretary Timothy Geithner is the only person known to have had extensive plastic surgery to make himself look uglier. Sick to death of being admired for his beauty and not his economic brains, Tim "Baywatch" Geithner (as he used to be known) paid over $259,000 to have his face surgically re-constructed to resemble that of the sniggering cartoon character Beavis (from *Beavis and Butthead*). This lends a poignant twist to his nomination last year as one of *People* magazine's top 50 beautiful people. Originally, this was ascribed to the fact that Geithner's brother is a vice president at *People*. In fact, however, it was a tribute by those who remembered just how crazily handsome Geithner used to be. Geithner, however, has no regrets. "The way women used me—it was disgusting. I was nothing more than a piece of meat to them."

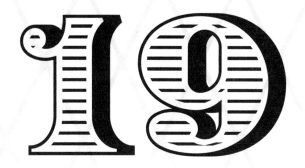

On Martin Luther King Day

ask why we have a public holiday named after a Vietcong-supporting radical who—in a 1967 speech—compared U.S. forces in Vietnam to Nazis. (True, by the way.) That ought to pull your liberal friend up short. If he recovers his wits and says MLK was right about Vietnam, tell him to talk to some Boat People. In the meantime, you'll celebrate Lee-Jackson Day, because Robert E. Lee and Stonewall Jackson were officers and gentlemen.

20

Next time you hear a reference to "America's first black president,"

counter by referring to Obama as "America's 44th white president." Explain that you're doing so on feminist grounds: "What? You're trying to tell me that his Caucasian mom's genetic input doesn't count? But that's so SEXIST!"

21

Tell them you don't give a damn about the polar bears.

And it's not because you don't like cute, fluffy, white carnivores; it's because you find it hard to accept that a species whose population has increased fivefold—from 5,000 to 25,000—in the last five decades can actually be in any kind of trouble.

22

Quote the wisdom of Al "Nature Watch" Gore:

. . . .

"A zebra does not change its spots."

Conservative history:

Explain how conservatives are the primary drivers of man's evolution. For instance, fire can only possibly have been discovered by a conservative unworried by liberal health and safety regulations. Moreover, by learning to cook meat, early man made it more digestible, meaning he had more energy available to develop not only his "brawnpower" but his brainpower. If *Homo Liberalis* had gotten his way, fire would have been banned as a dangerous substance, and we'd still be living in the trees, chewing natural, healthy, raw vegetables, burping contentedly, and being ruled by a loud, gossipy matriarchy of Oprahs and Streisands.

24

Tell your liberal friends you prefer foreign policy Teddy Roosevelt style:

. . . .

"Speak softly and carry a big stick"

to foreign policy Barack Obama style:

. . . .

"Speak softly, bow deeply, and apologize often."

Conservative party trick:

Say: "Mind if I smoke?" Then explain you've felt much more comfortable asking this question ever since you learned that "passive smoking" is a big government lie designed by safety Nazis to justify their persecution of tobacco users. The biggest long-term study of "passive smoking" found that exposure to "environmental tobacco smoke," no matter how intense or prolonged, creates no significantly increased risks of heart disease or lung cancer. Then go further. Spread the rumor that it is only through the assiduous efforts of smoking that America has enough cloud cover to deflect the apocalyptic effects of global warming.

Sing

"I've got the brains, you've got the looks—let's make lots of money," from the Pet Shop Boys' song "Opportunities (Let's Make Lots of Money)." Then ask why liberals can't understand basic economic principles like the division of labor, Ricardo's theory of comparative advantage, and Adam Smith's paean to free trade in *The Wealth of Nations* when they're simple enough to be summed up in one line of a dumb 1980s dance hit.

27

Start a rumor:

· ·

The now notorious and apparently crazy liberal group ACORN (the Association of Community Organizations for Reform Now) was actually a black ops front organization, devised during the Nixon era to discredit the Left. Its greatest victory came in 2009 when conservative activists videoed ACORN employees advising on how best to run a child-prostitution ring while avoiding taxes. You don't think even a left-wing, "social justice" organization could be that dumb, do you? It was all part of the plan. *The CIA's plan.*

28

Give them another reason why Obama has GOT to go.

. . . .

NO. 2.

He's a Muslim extremist. Witness his disastrous Cairo speech, in which he toadied to the worst elements of Islam—and betrayed the moderate elements—a) by referring to the 9/11 killers not as "terrorists," but as "violent extremists"; b) by pandering to the notion that there is an Islamic global community ("Ummah") set apart from the rest of the world; c) by apologizing on the West's behalf for the (defensive) Crusades; and d) by announcing that it wasn't the business of the United States to decide which countries can and can't have nuclear weapons (so go right ahead, Mister Ahmadinejad)....
Oh—did anyone mention this before?—and his middle name is Hussein, and he made one of NASA's top priorities an outreach program to make Muslims feel good about Islam's alleged contributions to science.

Diss *Avatar* (method 1).

Liberals love *Avatar*. It's the film with everything: oppressed native peoples; a disabled hero; mixed-race (actually mixed-species, even better) romance; dumb, probably Republican-voting baddies coming unstuck; Mother Gaia in the form of a pretty, shiny tree; an environmentalist theme. Therefore, never refer to the film as *Avatar*; instead, use the title of *South Park*'s horribly accurate parody: *Dances with Smurfs*.

Instead of using the term "liberal,"

why not try "libtard"? It's apt (liberal + retard = libtard), it's highly offensive, and quite deliciously un-PC. What's not to like?

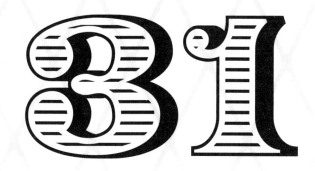

Quote Auberon Waugh:

"The urge to pass new laws must be seen as an illness, not much different from the urge to bite old women. Anyone suspected of suffering from it should either be treated with the appropriate pills or, if it is too late for that, elected to parliament [or Congress, as the case may be] and paid a huge salary with endless holidays, to do nothing whatever."

32

When Black History Month (formerly known as February) begins,

always refer to it as Fake History Month. Then explain that you refuse to support a racist event which essentially demeans African Americans by subtly implying that they are too bigoted and dumb to relate to any historical event which doesn't involve people with the right skin tone.

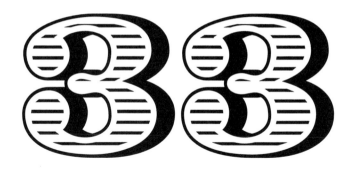

33

Start a rumor:

Only a fraction of Bono's vast fortune comes from record sales and touring. His real money-spinner is the child labor sweatshops he owns in Southeast Asia, which manufacture more than 47 percent of Nike's product range.

34.

Global Warming Fun.

NO. 2.

Never let a cold day go by without reiterating: "Brrr. Still cold. Makes you think what we could really do with right now is a bit more *global warming*."

35

Deploy the *Reductio ad Hitleram.*

NO. 2.

"Hey, you're a vegetarian! Has anyone ever told you Hitler was too?" (They will have heard this. All too frequently.) The veggie will probably respond by telling you that this is an urban myth and that Hitler did occasionally eat meat. In fact, the urban myth is literal fact, as we know from *Hitler's Table Talk.* Not only did Hitler think that vegetarianism was doing the "right thing" by the animal kingdom (Hitler was a leader in "animal rights"), but he was certain that the future belonged to vegetarians. The real urban myth is the veggie's fanatically spread tale about how Hitler really wasn't a committed veggie.

On Ronald Reagan's birthday
(February 6), quote him:

"The nine most terrifying words in the English language are: 'I'm from the government and I'm here to help.'"

Conservative movies:

BRAZIL (1985)

Celebrate Terry Gilliam's dystopian fantasy *Brazil* as a parable of just how unspeakably horrible things get when the liberals take charge: insane bureaucracy; universal police surveillance; state-sponsored torture; terrorism; a heartless elite; a labyrinthine government machine from which the only possible escape is the solace of insanity....And Gilliam had never even heard of Rahm Emanuel when he made it.

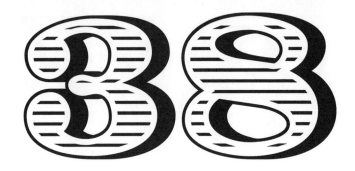

Use Joseph Schumpeter's birthday (February 8) as an excuse to explain exactly what was wrong with Obama's "Porkulus" package.

Using taxpayers' money to prop up failing industries that the market no longer deems viable is a classic socialist error: what a healthy economy really needs is Schumpeter's "creative destruction," whereby the death of an old industry creates space for the birth of a new industry, which in turn generates more money and more jobs. Explain that the reasons socialists like Obama hate this process are a) they can't control it, and b) it works.

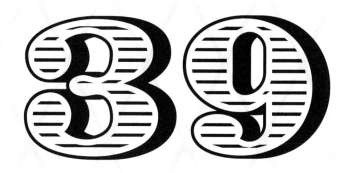

39

On his birthday (February 9), quote Thomas Paine, who foresaw 250 years ago just where the United States could go wrong:

"Government, even in its best state, is but a necessary evil; in its worst state, an intolerable one."

40

Start a rumor:

The arrest of Henry Louis Gates in Cambridge, Massachusetts, was in fact part of a vicious turf war among African American Studies academics who are split into two rival gangs: Oreos and Panthers. The man who called the police when Gates was trying to get into his own home was none other than black radical academic Cornel West, hoping to start a gang war to liven things up in the ivory (isn't that prejudiced?) tower.

41

Give them another reason why Obama has GOT to go.

NO. 3.

He claimed to have campaigned "in 57 states—I think one left to go"; he referred to a Navy corpsman as a "corpse-man"; and in a speech in France, he seemed to think "American" was a language. Need I go on?

Praise Joe Biden, historian, by quoting him:

"When the stock market crashed, Franklin D. Roosevelt got on the television and didn't just talk about the, you know, princes of greed. He said, 'Look, here's what happened.'"

The stock market crashed in 1929. FDR was elected in 1932. And televisions were still in the laboratory.

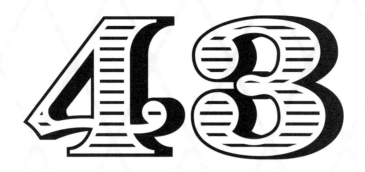

43

Tell a joke:

Q: Why do liberals like smart women?

A: Opposites attract.

Pick a fight with a liberal on:

CAPITALISM.

Agree with *Wall Street*'s Gordon Gekko that "greed—for want of a better word—is good." Explain wearily but patiently to a liberal that firms can only gain revenue by selling things that people want; and only make a profit if they sell these things for more than they cost to produce. In the process they give employment to people who prefer that job to any other they can find. Therefore, profit-making firms create wealth for their customers, owners, and employees. They take wealth from no one. So why, pray, do liberals have such a problem with capitalism?

Praise the down-to-earth, regular Joe qualities of Barack Obama, who claims to remain a huge fan of his old home team the Chicago White Sox.

So much so that when interviewed about his enthusiasm in April 2010, he couldn't name anyone who played for the Sox when he was growing up, nor did he know how to pronounce the name of the Sox's famous Comiskey Park.

46

Go hunting polar bears in Nunavut.

Spend the rest of your life happily regaling liberals with every last detail of your adventure. Say: "But you know it's really a form of aboriginal ecotourism. The Inuit depend for their livelihoods on organized sports hunting. So I was just doing my bit for the environment and the cause of native peoples. Maybe you'd like to try it? I can give you a contact number…"

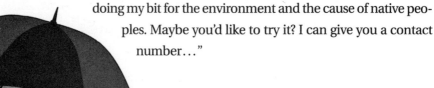

47

Pick a fight with a liberal on:

SOCIAL JUSTICE.

"Social justice" is an entirely arbitrary concept that could only exist in the warped brains of *bien-pensant* compulsive meddlers. The correct response is "Whose social justice?" An NAACP activist's definition of "social justice" might well differ from that of a KKK member; an eco-campaigner's view of "social justice" will surely be different from that of someone from the Competitive Enterprise Institute. It is entirely typical of the sublime arrogance and blinkered bigotry of liberals that they imagine their version of "social justice" is the correct one. This, in itself, is more than reason enough to show why liberals should never be allowed anywhere near state office.

Next time a liberal talks about "social justice," tell him you'll take your "justice" straight up, without any prefixes, as established in a rule of law based on Christian principles in a democratic state, and see how he gets out of that.

48

Tell a joke:

Q: Why is it so hard for liberals to make eye contact?

A: Obama's rear doesn't have eyes.

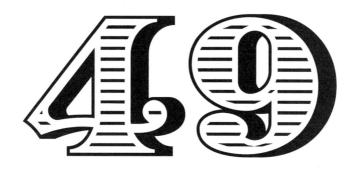

Praise Chilean dictator General Augusto Pinochet.

Sure, like his Commie predecessor Salvador Allende, he had his faults, but his economic legacy has made Chile the richest per-capita, healthiest, least corrupt country in South America. Liberals hate being told this. Their hero is the "martyred" Allende. But under Allende, inflation was running at 1,000 percent, whereas thanks to free market reforms introduced by Pinochet—taking advice from Milton Friedman's "Chicago Boys"—the Chilean economy thrived. We saw the results of this from two earthquakes—the one in Haiti in January 2010 that claimed nearly a quarter of a million lives; and the one in Chile a month later which, though 500 times more powerful, claimed just over 700 lives. Why? Because rich

CONTINUED ON NEXT PAGE

CONTINUED FROM PREVIOUS PAGE

economies can afford to build earthquake-proof buildings. But impoverished ones dependent for their survival on international aid can't.

Postcript: When Milton Friedman collected his Nobel Prize, he was heckled by leftists for having advised so repugnant a regime. He wryly noted that he had given Communist dictatorships the same advice—but strangely no one attacked him for that.

50

Quote the wisdom of Lurve Poodle Al Gore:

"We're all capable of mistakes, but I do not care to enlighten you on the mistakes we may or may not have made."

51

On his birthday (February 22), quote George Washington as a reminder that, from first to last, all of America's greatest presidents have believed above all in liberty:

· ·

"Government is not reason; it is not eloquence; it is force. Like fire, it is a dangerous servant and a fearful master."

52

Start a rumor:

REM's 1991 hit "Losing My Religion" was a veiled, deeply personal account by singer/songwriter Michael Stipe of how it feels, after a lifetime as a Democrat, suddenly to realize that your liberal ideals are a crock and you've been a secret conservative all your life. Stipe has been a closeted member of the Republican Party since 1991 and is in fact chairman of the highly secretive Republicans for Rock branch, whose membership allegedly also includes Ted Nugent, Snoop Dogg, Brandon Flowers, Lady Gaga, and Jon Bon Jovi. The personal happiness he has experienced as a result of his change of political heart has unfortunately resulted in a dramatic falling-off in the quality of his music. Artists need pain and misery to produce great work. It is no coincidence that REM's classic *Automatic for the People* album was recorded while Stipe was involved in a bitter power struggle with the late Gianni Versace for the presidency of the National Rifle Association (Gay Men's Branch).

Quote George Bernard Shaw:

. . . .

"A government that robs Peter to pay Paul can always depend on the support of Paul."

Defend the Crusades

. . . .

as an entirely reasonable response to centuries of Muslim persecution of Christians in the Holy Land, including the crucifixion and execution of pilgrims, and the plunder and destruction of churches—10,000 of them in the early eleventh century, including Jerusalem's Church of the Holy Sepulcher, the traditional site of Christ's burial.

55

Tell a joke:

Q: Why was Obama staring at the frozen orange juice can?

A: It said, "Concentrate."

56

Give them another reason why Obama has GOT to go.

NO. 4.

His speeches are SO boring. Remember all that pre-election propaganda about him being the greatest presidential orator since Abraham Lincoln? Yeah, right. Maybe on the first few listens that gravelly, ponderous, measured style might have fooled us into thinking he had something to say. But he doesn't. Just airy platitudes, colossal egoism, and fake profundity such as, "We do not have to think that human nature is perfect for us to still believe that the human condition can be perfected." Yeah, whatever, Barack. Zzzzzz.

57

Campaign on behalf of American blacks for reparations from the wicked West African country of Ghana.

After all, it was the native Ashanti kings who were the middle men for the African slave trade.

Suggested outfits to wear to a Palestine fundraiser:

Him: blond, sticking-up, Geert Wilders fright wig.

Her: transparent black dress, naked body decorated with Koranic verses, as featured in the Ayaan Hirsi Ali movie *Submission*.

Conservative party trick:

When served vegetarian food, politely ask if they wouldn't mind rustling you up a meat dish. Explain apologetically, "It's a dietary problem I have. I just can't eat anything that doesn't have eyes."

Some liberals have actually been shocked at the radical drift of Mr. Hope and Change.

If your friend is one of these, make him a gift basket of aroma-therapeutic candles, a CD of healing nature sounds, and a copy of *Welcome to Obamaland*, and perhaps the light will finally dawn. If that doesn't work, buy a boom box and do break dances on your driveway while listening to Rush Limbaugh really loud.

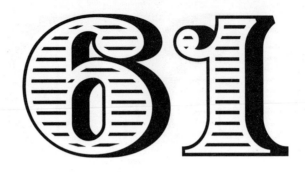

Attack a liberal icon:

If you see a liberal wearing a Che Guevara t-shirt, say: "Yeah, when I was a kid I thought I was cool and outrageous wearing a Charles Manson t-shirt—until my mom and dad told me exactly the sick things he'd done. I guess you never learned that your sicko mass murderer Che killed way more people than my mass murderer did."

Boycott rock fundraisers (Live Aid; Live 8; etc).

Explain that rock stars have an unerring ability to choose the wrong causes. The original Live Aid event, for example, might have killed at least as many Africans as it saved by encouraging Ethiopia's Marxist dictator Mengistu Haile Mariam in the Stalinist "land reform" program that had caused the famine in the first place.

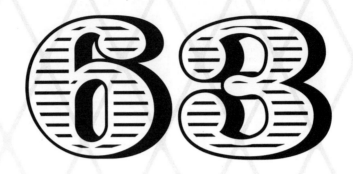

Launch a campaign to
DESTROY THE
AMAZON RAINFOREST.

Tell your liberal friend that it's growing so fast there's a danger that within a few decades it might reach the southern borders of the United States, menacing our great-grandchildren with its evil leafy tendrils and its deadly population of jaguars, bullet ants, snakes, killer bees, and such like. You think we exaggerate? According to a January 2009 report in the *New York Times*—and what liberal could ignore the voice of *Pravda*?—"For every acre of rainforest cut down each year, more than 50 acres are growing." Do the math. Then be afraid. Very afraid. And start stockpiling the Agent Orange.

64.

Give them another reason why Obama has GOT to go.

NO. 5.

He doesn't think America's anything special. No really, he doesn't. Quote: "I believe in American exceptionalism, just as I suspect the Brits believe in British exceptionalism and the Greeks believe in Greek exceptionalism." In other words: everybody's special. Tell your friend that, with his Barney the Dinosaur egalitarian worldview of everybody being special, Obama ought to be a kindergarten teacher, leading the kids in non-competitive, non-judgmental songs, not the leader of the free world.

65

Global Warming Fun.

NO. 3.

Note that it is *still* cold. Remark on this fact to liberals. Say: "Hey, do you remember the time when all those liberal, ecotard crazies used to tell us we were all going to fry because of 'Global Warming'? How dumb must they be feeling now?"

Next time a liberal touts to you the virtue of this or that government program,

tell him that we should never encourage governments to create new programs, because it really just encourages them to beggar us all. Quote Adam Smith: "There is no art which one government sooner learns of another than that of draining money from the pockets of the people." Tell your liberal friend that taxation is essentially theft by big bully government; you're for power to the people.

67

Tell a joke:

Q: What do you call a thousand liberals at the bottom of the sea?

A: A good start.

Conservative movies:
Red Dawn (1984)

The Russians invade (or, if it's the rumored upcoming remake, the Chinese), and the U.S. president—a sonorous-voiced, African American lawyer who cut his teeth in the Chicago political machine—knows exactly what to do: surrender, negotiate, and be pleasantly surprised by how much room there is for partnership with the wonderful, enlightened new regime. No, not really. John Milius's film was made in the Reagan era, and it shows. America fights back. To the bitter end. If cute Jennifer Grey has to rig herself up to a booby-trapped grenade so she takes at least one of the Red sons-of-bitches with her, such is the price of liberty. God bless America. Better dead than red.

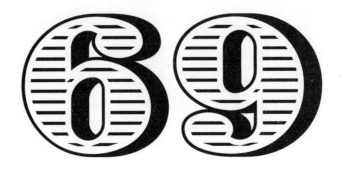

Start a rumor:

The reason Obama's enviro-czar Carol Browner is such a superbly accomplished liar is that she practices every day in front of her three cats Lysenko, Malthus, and Pol Pot.

Sympathize most deeply with the tragedy of Michelle "Lady Macbeth" Obama,

who, thanks to the oppressive white male hegemony against which she so rightly rails, has been constantly thwarted and frustrated in her arduous rise from Princeton to Harvard to prestigious law firms to the black D.C. ghetto in which she now resides. Say: "She's angry and she has EVERY right to be!"

71

Express outrage that there are *still* people out there so foolish as to deny the existence of Anthropogenic Global Warming (AGW).

After all, among those who just *know* AGW to be true are some of the most important thinkers of our age: Leonardo DiCaprio, Paris Hilton, Ed Begley Jr., and Arnie Schwarzenegger. And who do the Climate Change deniers have in their camp, pray? Why, only complete nobodies like Professor Richard Lindzen, atmospheric physicist at MIT; professor and atmospheric physicist Fred Singer of the University of Virginia; Dr. Roy Spencer, a climatologist who used to work for NASA; Dr. Willie Soon, an astrophysicist at the Harvard-Smithsonian Center for Astrophysics…

72

Diss *Avatar* (method 2):

Annoy liberals by praising it as one of the greatest libertarian parables ever made. The Na'vi people, like all good conservatives, cherish their God-given landscape. The film is about the battle to protect their property rights against a sinister governmental machine that tries ruthlessly to steal from them. All hail James Cameron: a truly great conservative filmmaker!

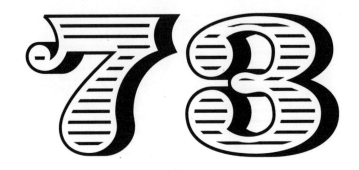

Conservative party piece:

Boast that you never allow your kids to watch network news or read the local liberal newspaper. When your liberal friend responds, "Then how are they going to learn about the world?" reply, "Oh, you know, with things called books. Right now they're reading *Animal Farm* and *The Road to Serfdom*."

Reclaim rock for conservatism:

Sing "California Uber Alles" by the Dead Kennedys, especially the lines:

> Zen fascists will control you
> 100% natural
> You will jog for the master race
> And always wear the happy face.

Then remark how spookily prescient it was that an obscure, left-ish, 1970s punk band managed to predict the eco-Nazi tyranny of Governor Arnold Schwarzenegger.

Never speak of "Healthcare reform."

....

Prefer "Healthcare takeover."

Apply to the
National Endowment for the Arts

· ·

for funding for a new art work in which you propose to photograph an image of Mohammad submerged in your own urine. When they refuse, complain: "Well, you didn't have any problems with Andres Serrano's 'Piss Christ,' did you?"

Instead of "Progressive," always use the words "Oppressive" or "Regressive."

· ·

When called on this, feign puzzlement. "But how is it progress to steal free citizens' liberties, money, and hope, and hand it all over to government bureaucrats?"

78

Tell a joke:

Q: What's the difference between a liberal and a puppy?

A: A puppy stops whining after it grows up.

Quote P. J. O'Rourke:

"The principal feature of American liberalism is sanctimoniousness. By loudly denouncing all bad things—war and hunger and date rape—liberals testify to their own terrific goodness. More important, they promote themselves to membership in a self-selecting elite of those who care deeply about such things.... It's a kind of natural aristocracy, and the wonderful thing about this aristocracy is that you don't have to be brave, smart, strong, or even lucky to join it, you just have to be liberal."

80

Deploy the *Reductio ad Hitleram.*

NO. 3.

"Hey, you're into organic food? Just like Heinrich Himmler! He was as crazy about it as you are! He had this great plan to feed the entire SS on nothing but organic food. Problem was organic food requires about four times as much land to produce as non-organic food and the Nazis just couldn't grab enough of it. Anyway, not being a Nazi myself I prefer to stick to non-organic food. It's cheaper, and it means there's more land to spare to feed the people who need it. You know, Third World people and *Untermenschen* like that."

81

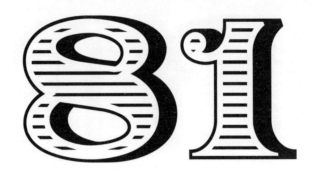

Tell a joke:

Q: What's the only thing worse than an incompetent liberal president?

A: A competent liberal president.

Start a rumor:

Kanye West is a Barry Goldwater nut. Though the rap star was not even born when Goldwater campaigned in the 1964 presidential election, he was introduced to his philosophy by fellow Goldwater enthusiast Ghostface Killah, who told him, "That Barry. He's my homie!" West owns the world's largest collection of Goldwater memorabilia (including 387 different lapel pins, over 3,000 posters, as well as the original megaphone used by Goldwater while addressing a crowd in Birmingham, Alabama). He has vowed never to support the Republican cause until a candidate emerges who is properly in tune with Goldwater's libertarian instincts.

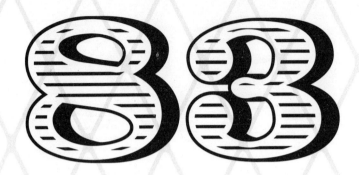

83

Tell your liberal neighbor that you're going to bury a "time capsule" box in your yard.

Explain that you're not going to dig it up until Obama leaves the White House in 2012, but that you're going to make a list now of the top ten excuses liberals are going to make for his abject failure. Then when you and your neighbor dig up the box, you can see how accurate your predictive powers are.

Write down: 1. Racism 2. Racism. 3. Racism. 4. Racism. 5. Racism. 6. . . .

Slaughter a liberal sacred cow:

Explain that China's "genocide" in Tibet is a liberal myth, eagerly stoked by the exiled Dalai Lama (who has no vested interests, right?) and funded in the 1950s by the CIA as part of a campaign to discredit the Communist Chinese. Most of the Tibetan monasteries were destroyed during the Cultural Revolution by young native *Tibetan* Communists convinced that religion had inhibited Tibet's modernization. Stories about mass killings turn out, on close scrutiny, to be entirely fictitious. Conclude this mini-history lesson by asking: "Anyway, what's your problem? You're a liberal. You LIKE Commies!"

85

Quote the wisdom of Al "Nostradamus" Gore:

"The heart of the security agenda is protecting lives—and we now know that the number of people who will die of AIDS in the first decade of the twenty-first century will rival the number that died in all the wars in all the decades of the twentieth century."

Conservative history:

Describe how, contrary to cozy liberal myth, the great FDR managed to prolong the Great Depression by seven years. Research by UCLA economists Harold L. Cole and Lee E. Ohanian has shown that the anti-competition and pro-labor measures Roosevelt signed into law as part of his New Deal stalled what could have been a "beautiful recovery."

87

Tell a joke:

· ·

Q: What do you get if you cross a crooked politician with a crooked lawyer?

A: Barack Obama.

88

Global Warming Fun.

NO. 4.

Pick a cold day in April to remind all the liberals you know how miserable the weather *still* is. Ask: "Do you think there's a single person left out there who's still stupid enough to believe in global warming?" If the liberal tries explaining to you the difference between "weather" and "climate," laugh darkly and cynically and go, "Yeah, right. When it's hot, the eco-nuts will tell you it's proof of dangerous climate change. But when it's cold, they tell you it's just 'weather'? How dumb do those tree-huggers think we are?"

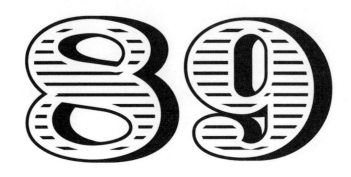

Ask a liberal, "Isn't *Team America: World Police* the greatest film in the history of world cinema?"

Do so only rhetorically, though, because the answer is obvious: yes, it is. Matt Stone's and Trey Parker's marionette masterpiece is greater than *Citizen Kane*, way funnier (and less Commie) than *The Battleship Potemkin*, and so patriotic it makes *The Birth of a Nation* look like *Avatar*. Some liberals like to kid themselves that the movie is a satire on gung-ho American imperialism. But that's just a ruse to take liberal money at the box office. This is the film that tells it like it is: the Middle East is full of terrorists, Hollywood actors like Alec Baldwin, Tim Robbins, and Sean Penn are all crypto-Communist fags in league with Kim Jong Il, and Michael Moore is evil incarnate. They all must die.

· ·365 WAYS TO DRIVE A LIBERAL CRAZY ·

90

Defend Israel.

LIBERAL MYTH NO. 1:

The Jews stole the land from the Palestinians.

REFUTATION:

No, they didn't. After the Romans cleared out and decimated the mighty cities built by Jews like King Herod, Palestine was an arid, sparsely populated backwater that was eventually claimed (for land bridge reasons) by the Ottoman Empire, then by the British Empire. Jews have lived in the region continuously

CONTINUED ON NEXT PAGE

CONTINUED FROM PREVIOUS PAGE

for well over 2,000 years. The British found themselves overseeing an indigenous population made up of Jews and Arabs—and sometimes Arab Jews. All were referred to as "Palestinians." Ownership of the land was a patchwork. Much of the land was owned by absentee landlords who lived in places like Egypt, and farmed by local Arab Palestinians. This may have made many Palestinians believe it was "their land," but sorry, that just wasn't the case. As the Zionist movement gained traction in the early 1900s, Jews around the world contributed to a fund to buy up tranches of land, and much of the land for the future Jewish state envisioned by the early Zionists was acquired this way. Once again, the poor Arabs living on and farming the land may not have been happy to give up the land they lived on, but it was not "stolen from them," because they didn't own it to begin with.

Turn up at your local Muslim outreach program

wearing an "I'd rather be Waterboarding" t-shirt.

92

Quote the wisdom of Al "Tim Berners Lee" Gore:

"During my service in the United States Congress, I took the initiative in creating the internet."

93

Pick a fight with a liberal on:

DIVERSITY.

Next time you're told that "diversity is our strength," ask how that worked out in Yugoslavia.

94.

Tell a liberal how much you admire the lofty neutrality and commitment to truth at all costs of their house journal the *New York Times*.

. . . .

NO. 1.

In the 1930s, *Times* reporter Walter Duranty acted as one of Stalin's "useful idiots" by praising the glorious achievements of Soviet communism, even to the extent of denying the existence of the Ukraine famine that killed millions.

95

Invite all your liberal friends to a Tax Freedom Day party.

Remind them that this is the first day of the year in which the money they work for goes into their own pockets rather than into Big Government's gaping, insatiable maw. In 2010 Tax Freedom Day fell on April 9. In 1900 it fell on January 22.

Say a prayer:

Dear Lord, you took my favorite actor Patrick Swayze. You took my favorite actress Farrah Fawcett. You took my favorite singer Michael Jackson. I just wanted to let you know that my favorite president is Barack Obama. Amen.

Say to a liberal:

"Yeah, I used to think that way before my frontal lobes had developed. You'll grow out of it." Elaborate by explaining that liberalism is the philosophy of the adolescent: whiny, insecure, full of big crazy ideas that have no practical application in the real world, and with a tragically inflated sense of entitlement.

98

Give them another reason why Obama's GOT to go.

. . . .

NO. 6.

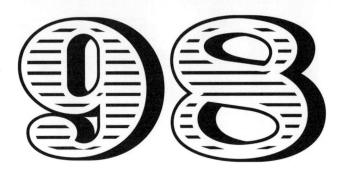

He's an ageist, sexist, racist. See, for instance, the video mailed in 2010 to Democratic activists: "It will be up to each of you to make sure that the *young people*, *African Americans*, *Latinos*, and *women*, who powered our victory in 2008, stand together once again." What? No gratitude to the 41 percent of white male voters who put him in the White House?

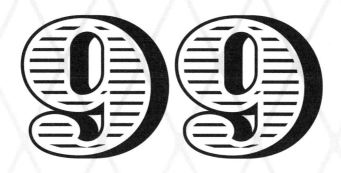

Conservative movies:

BLACK HAWK DOWN (2001)

Rejoice in the political incorrectness of *Black Hawk Down* where, for a body count of 19 Americans, at least 1,000 Somali jihadis are mown down by super-trained and disciplined Army Rangers. Then quote George S. Patton: "No bastard ever won a war by dying for his country. He won it making the other poor dumb bastard die for his country."

100

Deploy the *Reductio ad Hitleram.*

. . . .

NO. 4.

When confronted with an animal rights fanatic, say, "Hey! You mean you're like Hermann Goering. Do you know that in 1933 he said that anyone found guilty of animal cruelty or experimentation would be sent to a con-centration camp? They really cared about animals, those Nazis!"

101

Whenever the mood takes you, call up liberal friends

and read them random chunks of *Newsweek*'s Evan Thomas's gushing response on MSNBC to the Obamessiah's Cairo surrender speech. Make them cringe and writhe with lines like: "I think the President's speech yesterday was the reason we Americans elected him. It was grand. It was positive. Hopeful.... But what I liked about the President's speech in Cairo was that it showed a complete humility.... The question now is whether the President we elected and spoke for us so grandly yesterday can carry out the great vision he gave us and to the world"; and "He's going to bring all different sides together.... Obama is trying to sort of temper everything down. He doesn't even use the word terror. He uses extremism. It's all about let us reason together.... He's the teacher. He's going to say, 'Now, children, stop fighting and quarreling with each other.' And he has a kind of moral authority that he—he can—he can do that."

102

Pick a fight with a liberal on:

JUDGMENT.

Liberals love accusing people of being "judgmental." And that's, like, what, supposed to be a BAD thing? If we don't teach our kids to make judgments—and fast—how are we ever going to stop them being fleeced or mugged every time they quit the front door? And how are we ever going to survive in business if we can't suss the difference between trustworthy clients and bad debtors? Our whole life is spent learning how to form judgments—between good and bad, right and wrong, nice and nasty. This is the basis of wisdom. But then a liberal would never understand that, wisdom being an entirely alien concept.

Agree wholeheartedly with the "Precautionary Principle."

Argue fervently for the passing of national laws enforcing the wearing of tin foil hats as a precaution against the possibility of aliens from outer space trying to control our minds. Argue too for a massive government spending program to build mighty death lasers at strategic points around the United States, so as to stave off possible alien invasion and/or asteroid strikes. Say: "It might never happen. But it's like global warming: the hazards in the very unlikely event that it IS true are so great, we simply CAN'T AFFORD NOT TO ACT!"

104

Agree wholeheartedly that "liberalism" is the only political philosophy any sane person could possibly hold.

Fulminate at length against the lunatics who oppose "liberalism": the scroungers, the malcontents, the life-haters, the losers, the crypto-Communists, the eco-fascists. Say: "I'm with you all the way, buddy. The sooner Big Government butts out of our lives, the better we'll all be...."

Quietly enjoy the liberal's growing discomfort as he realizes your views are diametrically opposed to his own. Then say: "Oh. You're *that* kind of liberal. I thought you meant you were a liberal in its original, true, classic, libertarian sense. Before it got hijacked by the Left..."

105

Make a liberal read former Colorado governor Richard D. Lamm's 2004 "I Have a Plan to Destroy America" speech.

The guy's a Democrat eco-nut, so they'll surely sympathize, initially, with what he has to say. Lamm says that if you wanted to destroy America, you would: 1. Make the United States a bilingual country. 2. Invent "multiculturalism." 3. Turn the United States into an "Hispanic Quebec." 4. Make America's fastest growing demographic group the least educated. 5. Encourage big business to

CONTINUED ON NEXT PAGE

fund campaigns to emphasize racial difference and celebrate the "cult of victi-mology." 6. Celebrate diversity. 7. Make it taboo to talk about these things and call anyone who tries to do so a "racist" or "xenophobe." 8. Ban Victor Davis Hanson's book *Mexifornia*, which exposes the details of Lamm's wicked plan.

Ask the liberal why he isn't laughing at Lamm's wonderful joke.

106

On Adolf Hitler's birthday (April 20), call up all your liberal friends to congratulate them.

When they express outrage, respond with deep surprise: "But I thought... well, I thought Hitler was kind of a role model for you socialists? He loved big government... and furry animals... and hated smoking... and thought we needed to get beyond restrictive Judeo-Christian morality... and was pro-Muslim..."

107

Oldies but goodies corner:

Remind a liberal that more people died in Teddy Kennedy's car than were killed at Three Mile Island.

108

Celebrate Earth Day (April 22)

by reminding liberals of all the whacko predictions made by environmentalists in 1970, the year the event was founded: a new Ice Age (*Newsweek*); a world "eleven degrees colder by the year 2000" (Kenneth Watt); by 1985 air pollution to reduce the amount of sunlight reaching earth by one half (*Life* magazine); by 1995 between 75 and 85 percent of all species to be extinct (Earth Day founder Gaylord Nelson); mass starvation (Earth Day organizer Denis Hayes). Say: "Thank you, thank you, Earth Day! If those 20 million hippies hadn't taken the day off work, we'd all be dead by now!"

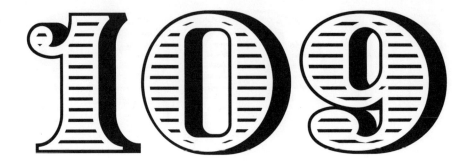

109

Spread a rumor:

. . . .

Mickey Mouse wears a Keith Olbermann watch.

110

If you are gay,

. . . .

always refer to your proclivity fondly as "my perversion"—or better still, when among your fellow gays, "Our perversion." Few things rile a liberal more than when a designated "victim" refuses to play identity politics.

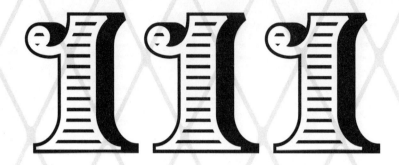

Tell a Nancy Pelosi joke:

A man washed up on a desert island after a shipwreck. The only other survivors were a sheep and a sheepdog.

The three of them got into the habit of going down to the beach every evening to watch the sunset.

One particular evening, the sky was a fiery red with beautiful cirrus clouds and the breeze was warm and gentle. It was a perfect night for romance. As they sat there, the sheep started looking better and better to the lonely man. Soon, he leaned over and put his arm around the sheep.

But the sheepdog, ever protective of the sheep, growled fiercely until the man backed away.

CONTINUED ON NEXT PAGE

CONTINUED FROM PREVIOUS PAGE

A few weeks passed by and, lo and behold, there was another ship-wreck. The only survivor was Nancy Pelosi.

That evening, the man took Nancy to watch the sunset. It was another beautiful tropical evening—perfect for romance. Before long the man started to get "those feelings" again.

He fought the urges as long as he could, but he finally gave in, moved closer to Nancy and told her he hadn't had sex for months.

Nancy batted her long, lovely eyelashes and asked if there was anything she could do to help.

"Yes," he said, "Take the dog for a walk."

(Joke hat tip: Ihatethemedia.com)

112

Call up a liberal friend in Connecticut anytime before, say, April 27,

and ask him how it feels to be living in the last state in the United States to reach Tax Freedom Day. Yep, that's right, you can say, every red cent anyone in Connecticut earns today will go straight into the gaping maw of big government. So who'd want to live in Connecticut—except maybe masochists, socialists, and people on welfare?

113

Just as you called your liberal friends on Adolf Hitler's birthday,

annoy the heck out of them by doing it again on the anniversary of Hitler's death (April 30) and offer your profound condolences.

When they get cross, tell them you feel their pain. As a conservative, you know how hard it is to be persecuted for holding views some find unfashionable. Say you won't condemn them for being socialist fellow travelers of Herr Hitler and that their secret is safe just so long as they agree not to try any of that Sieg Heil stuff when your kids are anywhere nearby.

Combat sexism:

. . . .

When playing mixed pairs golf, show solidarity with feminist players by insisting that men and women tee off from the same spot. Explain that you are doing your bit to combat the outrageous, phallocentric calumny that women are too weak to hit small spherical objects as far as men.

115

Quote Joe Biden on Barack Obama:

"I mean, you got the first mainstream African-American who is articulate and bright and clean and a nice-looking guy."

116

Always refer to greenies

like Al Gore, Carol Browner, and Ed Begley Jr. as "Watermelons"—
green on the outside, red on the inside.

Quote terrorist-turned-professor Bill Ayers:

"Everything was absolutely ideal on the day I bombed the Pentagon. The sky was blue. The birds were singing. And the bastards were finally going to get what was coming to them."

Then say: "Great prose style. You can see why his next book, *Dreams from My Father*, sold so well..."

118

Invite your liberal friends to a theme party

in which you serve moussaka, pork kebabs, taramasalata, and tomato and feta salad, all washed down with Retsina, accompanied by bouzouki music.

Conclude the evening with a ritual smashing of plates. Explain that the party is in honor of Barack Obama's spending policies. Already America's national debt exceeds $13 trillion. So who needs to fly on expensive summer vacations to the Mediterranean any more? Carry on like Obama is, and it really won't be long now before America *is* Greece.

119

Give them another reason why Obama's GOT to go.

NO. 7.

His wife is a woman who wasn't proud to be American until her husband became a front runner in the Democratic primaries during his 2008 presidential run. Was there ever a bigger case of liberal whining, persecution complex, myopia, narcissism, and inflated sense of entitlement?

120

Pick a fight with a liberal on Friedrich Hayek's birthday (May 8).

Quote him: "The basis of [the classical liberal] argument is that nobody can know who knows best and that the only way by which we can find out is through a social process in which everybody is allowed to try and see what he can do." Exactly! This shows up the rottenness at the core of all liberal arguments: built into them is the assumption that liberals know what is best for us. But they don't. If they did, how do you explain the fact that we're now being run by the Obama administration?

Defend Israel.

LIBERAL MYTH NO. 2:

It's an Apartheid State.

REFUTATION:

Yeah, so that'll be why Arabs serve in the Israeli parliament as MPs (known as MKs for "Members of Knesset"); why they serve in the Israeli foreign service, in the government ministries, and even—in the case of the Druze sect who are not seen as having divided loyalties—in the Israeli Defense Force. Most signs are written in Hebrew and Arabic. An Arab woman has more rights in Israel than in most countries in the Arab and Muslim world.

122

Global Warming Fun.

NO. 5.

At the first hint of warm weather, greet all your liberal friends with a frenzied "Aiiieeee! Aiiieeee!" while gesturing in terror at the mysterious glowing orb in the sky: "It's getting warmer!" If the liberal drily tells you that it probably has something to do with spring, say: "You mean, climate can change, like *naturally* without it being our fault? Why does nobody *mention* this stuff?"

123

Cite Vladimir Illich Lenin as evidence of why it makes sense to home-school your kids:

"Give me four years to teach the children and the seed I have sown will never be uprooted."

124

Deploy the *Reductio ad Hitleram*.

NO. 5.

To a Green: ""Hey! So you must be a big fan of Hitler's Germany. No one was greener than those Nazis. They were the first nation to take eco-protection seriously with their Reich Nature Protection Law of 1935; the first to think up the idea of a clean air act (though they could never get it to work—maybe it was those ovens that were the problem); the first to recognize how vital it was for Big Government to police every tiny detail of the nation's dietary habits. Personally I think I might have found all that Eco-Nazism a bit oppressive. But if that's the kind of thing that rocks your boat, well who am I to judge?"

125

Give them another reason why Obama has GOT to go.

NO. 8.

He has killed whatever was left of the "Special Relationship" by repeatedly stabbing America's most loyal ally, Britain, in the back: returning the Winston Churchill bust; snubbing a visiting British Prime Minister with a gift of a box of crappy DVDs (when in return Obama got a really thoughtful present: an ornamental pen-holder made from the timbers of the Victorian anti-slave ship HMS *Gannet*); stoking up further anti-Brit resentment by referring constantly to the multinational BP as "*British* Petroleum"—a name it hasn't used in over a decade.

Say you're trying to fly as much as possible this year so as to increase your Carbon Footprint.

When the liberal turns red and accuses you of killing the planet, reply: "Say WHAT? Of course carbon dioxide is good. Carbon dioxide is plant food. The more of it we have the better stuff grows and more people we can feed using less land. You have a problem with that? You, what, want Africans to starve or something?"

127

Quote the wisdom of Al "unpopular" Gore:

"The presidency is more than just a popularity contest."

128

Explain to a liberal the *real* reason why Democrats are so keen to reintroduce the Fairness Doctrine.

Because liberals make such uninspiring radio broadcasters, the only way they'll ever get commercial airtime is by government diktat. Almost every popular broadcaster is a conservative: Rush Limbaugh, G. Gordon Liddy, Michael Savage, Bill O'Reilly, Laura Ingraham, Sean Hannity, Glenn Beck, Mark Levin....The long and undistinguished list of liberals who have had their radio shows cancelled due to lack of listener interest includes ex-New York mayor Ed Koch, ex-California governor Jerry Brown, Harvard law professor Alan Dershowitz, actress Janeane Garofalo, ex-presidential candidate Gary Hart...

129

Praise the enlightened attitudes of those nice, caring Palestinians in Hamas—who recently banned women from riding motorcycles.

Clearly their motivation is to protect the fairer sex from the myriad dangers associated with this most risky form of transport. No wonder liberal Americans prefer Gaza's gentle, sensitive feminist government to that of Israel, whose government callously treats its women folk as if they were no different from men. Why, Israeli women are even allowed to disport themselves in revealing swimwear on the beach, exposing themselves to the lascivious stares of men

CONTINUED ON NEXT PAGE

CONTINUED FROM PREVIOUS PAGE

who might at any stage come up to them and say "Hi!" and invite them for a drink, with goodness knows what terrible potential consequences. Much better to live in Gaza, where the religious police protect girls from such horrors by giving them a sound beating if they are found improperly dressed!

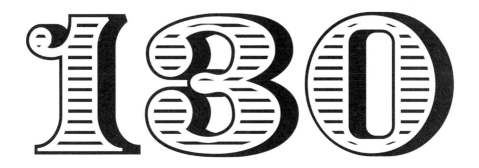

130

Anagram corner: President Barack Obama—Arab base, pink Democrat.

President Barack Hussein Obama—A Democrat speaks inane rubbish.

131

Quote Norman Thomas (U.S. socialist presidential candidate) on the true evils of liberalism:

"The American people will never knowingly adopt socialism. But, under the name of 'liberalism,' they will adopt every fragment of the socialist program, until one day America will be a socialist nation, without knowing how it happened."

132

Remark that it would be more than your life is worth to call Muhammad a "pedophile."

Explain that, of course, you understand that in seventh century Arabia when the Prophet married nine-year-old Aisha, child marriage was considered an entirely normal, healthy thing; who are we to judge to other cultures?

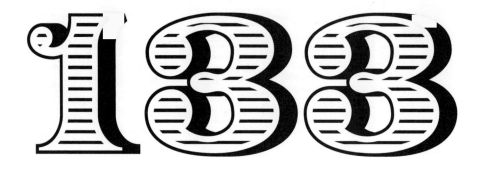

133

Serenade them with Ted Nugent's "Kiss My Ass,"

in which Mr. Nugent ventures a characteristically subtle and insightful critique of liberal values, to wit:

Kiss my ass—Callin' on Jesse Jackson

Kiss my ass—How about the IRS . . .

Kiss my ass—United Nations

Kiss my ass—All those Liberals

134

Tell a joke:

Q: Why is the healthcare plan called Obamacare, not Obamacares?

A: Because he doesn't.

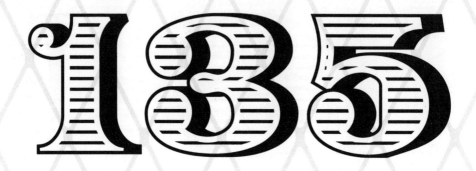

135

Find a feminist and see if she has a sense of humor:

Q: How many men does it take to open a beer?

A: None. It should be open when she brings it to you.

136

Conservative party tricks:

Say: "I guess I'm more of a libertarian than a conservative." Then see how extreme you can go before the liberal screams halt. Start with apparently socially liberal things they might like, "Yeah, I'm absolutely opposed to censorship," and then say, "I think hardcore porn should be available on network television if people want it, don't you?" Or say, "Yeah, I'm for legalizing drugs," and then say, "especially PCP and crack and drugs that target inner city young people, because if anyone needs to go tripping to escape their circumstances, it's them right?" You surely won't get beyond, "Yeah, and I'm for privatizing public schools." Liberals may be for some crazy things—but what liberal would dare to say that all schools should like, you know, compete for soundness; cater to parents rather than teachers unions and educrats; and be free instead of controlled by the state?

137

Pick a fight with a liberal on:

DISCRIMINATION.

In the days of the Founding Fathers, discrimination would have been the mark of a well-rounded, intelligent citizen. "Discrimination" meant "discernment"—an ability to make nice judgments about what was good, what was bad, what was mediocre, what was fake, what was genuine. Today it means "being unpleasant to women, ethnic minorities, gay people, and the disabled." So it is that another fine and quintessentially conservative concept has been hijacked and corrupted by the liberal Left to advance its agenda of resentment, bitterness, and slavering entitlement.

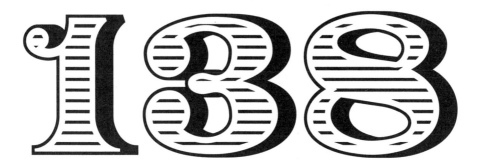

Say your personal liberal heroes are Ralph Nader and Michael Moore:

Without their help, the 2000 presidential election would have been won by Al Gore.

139

Refer freely and interchangeably to "liberals," "socialists," "Reds," "progressives," "Commies," "left-wing bastards," "pinkos," "Trots," "Nazis," etc.

When a liberal tries pointing out that some are more extreme than others, cut him short by quoting Dr. Johnson: "Sir, there is no settling the point of precedency between a louse and a flea."

140

Ask which part of this simple statement by Thomas Jefferson the Obama administration finds so hard to understand:

. . . .

"A wise and frugal government which shall restrain men from injuring one another, which shall leave them otherwise free to regulate their own pursuits of industry and improvement, and shall not take from the mouth of labor the bread it has earned. This is the sum of good government."

141

Quote the wisdom of Al "I have a dream" Gore:

"Verbosity leads to unclear, inarticulate things."

142

Give them another reason why Obama has GOT to go.

NO. 9.

He's unconstitutional. The bunch of crypto-Marxists, eco-Nazis, 9/11 Truthers, socialists, and radical agitators he has appointed as his "czars" are in clear violation of the Founding Fathers' principles. The czars have been granted the power of "principal officers" and ought therefore be subject to a confirmation vote by the Senate; or, if they are inferior officers, they should be answerable to Congress. The appointment of so many democratically unaccountable stooges represents a power grab that demonstrates Obama's utter contempt for the checks and balances that have preserved America from tyranny.

143

Tutor a liberal's kids in the ways of conservative righteousness—Lesson 1.

Make them watch *The Incredibles*—a celebration of courage, responsibility, marriage, achievement, and the family. Key scene is the one where Dash, the boy whose superpower is to run really fast, wants to try out for track but Mom says it wouldn't be fair. "Dad says our powers make us special!" protests Dash. "Everyone is special," says Mom, to which Dash mutters "Which means nobody is!" Over pizza and Coke afterwards, encourage your kids and the liberal's kids to empathize with Dash's rage. Explain: "And that, kids, is why if you hear your teacher saying elitism is bad he's telling you evil lies. The goal in life is to be the best at what you're good at—*not* to make everyone equal."

144

Brag that you often travel by private jet.

Not only will this make you sound important, but when the liberal splutters about your carbon footprint, cite the Leonardo DiCaprio defense: "There are situations within my industry where I have to get to someplace during a time frame where it's impossible to fly commercial."

145

Start a rumor:

Obama's regulatory czar Cass Sunstein has used the profits from his bestselling book *Nudge* to create what is believed to be the world's first private animal courtroom. With the help of top Hollywood animal wranglers, he has trained an orangutan to act as judge, a rare mountain gorilla to act as the top hotshot defense attorney, a chimpanzee to lead the prosecution, and an entire colony of bonobo monkeys to sit on the jury. Each weekend, Sunstein invites one of his human friends round to act as "defendant." Rumor has it that when Sunstein describes it as "just a game. Nothing serious. You don't really believe that I think primates should be conducting trials of humans, do you?" his voice takes on a manic, demented quality which some of his volunteers have said is "Really kinda scary."

146

Global Warming Fun.

. . . .

NO. 6.

On a hot summer's day, invite your closest liberal friends 'round for dinner—
with the air conditioning turned off. Explain you are trying to acclimatize to the
coming era, as planned for by the Environmental Protection Agency's and
Obama's enviro (energy and climate) czar Carol Browner,
in which the government will be able to control how
much electricity you use, especially in regards to
idle luxuries like air conditioning. Say: "Knowing
how you support the EPA's aims, I thought you guys
would appreciate the chance to *share* with me. . . ."

Scoff at the urban myth that the Muslims invented the zero.

Sure, mathematician Abu Ja'far Muhammad ibn Musa al-Khwarizmi was hugely influential in spreading the word, but the principles upon which he worked were discovered years before Muhammad. What we call Arabic numerals actually come from pre-Islamic India. Tell your liberal friend that what the Muslims actually invented was not the zero, but in fact zero—except for a few cultural traditions (like harems) that are quite nice for the oppressive male patriarchy.

148

Use air quotes when talking about "Islamophobia."

. . . .

Quote Roger Kimball's view that a "phobia" is an irrational fear and that there's nothing irrational about fearing a religion with a worryingly high proportion of adherents who think they're entirely justified blowing up innocent travelers and decapitating captured Westerners for the greater glory of Allah.

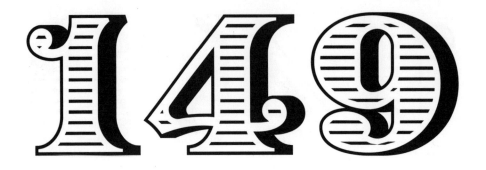

149

Name the three shortest books in the world:

· ·

How to Win Friends and Influence People by Rahm Emanuel; *Humility and Its Virtues* by Barack Obama; *What the Constitution Means to Me* by Nancy Pelosi.

Quote Abraham Lincoln:

. . . .

"Property is the fruit of labor. Property is desirable, is a positive good in the world. That some should be rich shows that others may become rich and hence is just encouragement to industry and enterprise. Let not him who is houseless pull down the house of another, but let him work diligently to build one for himself, thus by example assuring that his own shall be safe from violence."

Defend Israel.

LIBERAL MYTH NO. 3:

The Great Apartheid Wall. Liberals get almost sexually aroused by the thought of the evil, Berlin-style wall that supposedly divides the fascistic Israelis from the innocent, peace-loving Palestinians. The news media routinely features the tiny percentage (only about 10 percent) of the wall that is made of concrete.

REFUTATION:

The rest of the "wall" is actually a rather flimsy-looking fence, made of what appears to be pre-fab sections of high grade plastic. It is made to be light precisely so it can be moved easily. Parts of it have been taken down where it is no longer

CONTINUED ON NEXT PAGE

CONTINUED FROM PREVIOUS PAGE

needed. Israel also has a very active justice system, and challenges to the fence's placement are constantly being considered. The fence has been moved many times in response to court decisions. Its effectiveness (suicide bombings within Israel have ceased almost completely since the fence was put in place) comes not from the bulk or the height of the fence, but because Israel's famous high-tech smarts have been applied to its design with it wired to capture sound and motion and arranged in such a way as to collect footprints.

152

Announce you've been boycotting Wikipedia ever since you discovered that its supposedly neutral entries have been hijacked by leftists and eco-fascists.

From now on you'll rely on the only online encyclopedia that tells it straight: Conservapedia.

153

Invite your liberal friends 'round for a Rosenberg Death Day Celebration Barbeque.

Gloatingly recall all the international Marxists from Jean Paul Sartre to Pablo Picasso who opposed their execution. Then point out that President Eisenhower was entirely vindicated in his decision to make the traitors Julius and Ethel fry: as the Soviet VENONA cables revealed, they had indeed sold America's atomic secrets to the world's most evil regime.

154

Ridicule the claim—made by the leftist think tank The New Economics Foundation in their Happy Planet Index—that Cubans are the 7th happiest people in the world.

Yeah, that's why so many of them risk being drowned or eaten by tiger sharks trying to get to the United States (whose people are apparently only the world's 114th happiest).

155

Remind your liberal friends of the statistic that if liberals donated as much blood as conservatives, America's blood supply would increase by 45 percent.

So conservatives, literally, are the life blood of America, while liberals—in the main—are a drain.

156

Make them watch the "Death Camp of Tolerance" episode of *South Park*.

This is the one where class teacher Mr. Garrison attempts to get himself fired for being gay by shoving the class gerbil Lemmiwinks into Mr. Slave's "tight ass." When the schoolchildren complain about this they are sent to a "Tolerance camp" where screaming SS-type guards force them to draw pictures of "people of all colors and creeds holding hands beneath a rainbow." Meanwhile, back at school, Mr. Garrison wins a Courageous Teacher Award for overcoming adversity. At the end, ask the liberal why he didn't laugh very much.

157

Start a rumor:

Former senator Arlen Specter is planning a political comeback but has switched party loyalties so many times that he has to take medication normally prescribed to victims of split personality disorder. Each morning he has an aide come to whisper in his ear: "Remember sir, thou art a Democrat."

Ask:

If socialism is so great, how come the suicide rate is so much higher in countries with socialized medicine, including Sweden, Switzerland, France, and Cuba?

In a teary voice, tell the story of how it was General Douglas MacArthur who turned the Japanese on to whale meat.

The Japs never used to touch the stuff until the American Occupation after the war when food was scarce and MacArthur decreed that all Japanese children should eat whale meat as a cheap source of protein. Pause for effect, dab your eyes with a handkerchief, then say: "Damn! Doesn't it just make you SO proud to be American? It's thanks to our noble example that the seven seas are now nearly 100 percent free of the Deadly Whale Menace."

160

Give them another reason why Obama has GOT to go.

NO. 10.

Just how economically illiterate—make that economically *suicidal*—do you have to be to launch the eye-wateringly expensive Obamacare program (not to mention the bailouts and the "stimulus" spending that's directed almost entirely to government workers—just what hard-pressed taxpayers need, more government workers to be kept wallowing in pork) in the midst of the biggest financial crisis America has seen since the 1930s? Just how does recklessly expanding America's debt to the point of near bankruptcy and raising taxes on the productive sector of the economy serve any useful purpose? No wonder economist Arthur Laffer is predicting a double-dip recession. The recovery won't begin till Obama is out of office—and never let a liberal try to tell you otherwise.

161

Deploy the *Reductio ad Hitleram.*

NO. 6.

Anti-Smoking fanatics: "Hey! I quite understand. You and Adolf Hitler both. Hitler *hated* smoking. He called it 'the wrath of the Red Man against the White man, vengeance for having been given hard liquor.' The Nazis were among the first to ban smoking in many public places, including on trams and buses and in Nazi party premises. Just like modern day California, really."

Reclaim the language
for conservatism:

Instead of Mainstream Media (MSM) talk about the OLM—Old Left Media.

163

Quote the great free marketeer Claude Frederic Bastiat on his birthday (June 30):

"Each of us has a natural right, from God, to defend his person, his liberty and his property."

164

Quote liberal hero Karl Marx:

"There is only one way to kill capitalism—by taxes, taxes, and more taxes."

165

Sing the praises of Wal-Mart, a great American success story.

Liberals hate Wal-Mart because it puts local Mom and Pop concerns out of business, ruthlessly cuts costs, and is driven by profit. Well no kidding! Why do you think its annual revenues—$500 billion—exceed the GDP of all but 18 of the world's 181 countries? Because people (liberals too) like to shop there. If they didn't, it would go out of business. That's how economics works! Oh, I forgot, you're a liberal, you don't understand that.

166

Boycott Harry Potter.

Explain your reasoning to a liberal: author J. K. Rowling has been a big donor to Britain's terrible socialistic Labor Party that has ruined Great Britain's economy (more than once) and massively curtailed individual freedom in the land of Magna Carta. Thus, putting money in Rowling's pockets is as bad as buying South African oranges at the height of Apartheid. Your conscience simply wouldn't allow you to contribute, in however small a way, to the kind of government that oppresses free people. They may be Limeys, but Limeys have rights too!

167

On Independence Day, quote Calvin Coolidge (whose birthday it is) to show the essential difference between a good and bad president:

"It is much more important to kill bad bills than to pass good ones."

168

Deliberately misconstrue the meaning of the movie *The Stepford Wives* (the 1975 version, preferably, but the 2004 if you must).

"You're telling me the ending was supposed to be shocking? No way, man. That film is a utopian fantasy. The wives are happy—they get to wear pretty dresses and bake nice cakes, like all women secretly want to do. The husbands are happy. What's not to like?"

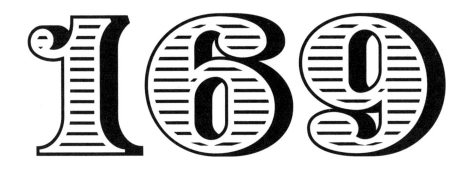

169

Quote Rush Limbaugh:

"Liberalism is hideous. It is the antithesis of being pro-human. It looks at life as a burden in and of itself to be managed, rather than as a blessing to be explored and lived to the fullest."

170

Global Warming Fun.

NO. 7.

On a beautiful hot summer's day, invite a liberal to crack open a can or two of ice cold beer by the pool. Say: "Run that Cap and Trade thing by me one more time because there's something I don't get. You guys are saying that we need to raise taxes and make energy more expensive so we can get *less* weather like this?"

171

When a liberal asks what you're buying your kids for their birthdays, say:

. . . .

"Oh, I guess the usual: more ammo."

172

Wrong-foot a liberal by appearing to agree with him on George W. Bush.

"Yeah I can't stand the guy either. Why the guy was almost as big a socialist as your Barack Obama. What kind of a conservative president allows the federal budget to grow on his watch from $1.2 trillion to $2.9 trillion? No kind of conservative president worthy of the name, that's for sure."

Defend Israel.

LIBERAL MYTH NO. 4:

"Israel was built by immigrants from European countries: they could 'go home' by going back to Germany, Austria, and Poland."

REFUTATION:

Baloney. More than half of Israel's Jewish population is of Arab stock and came to Israel when forced to leave Arab/Muslim countries like Morocco, Libya, Somalia, Ethiopia, Lebanon, Iraq, Syria, and Yemen.

Destroy a liberal's argument by exposing the underlying rhetorical cheat.

NO. 1.

Argumentum ad Verecundiam, otherwise known as the "argument from authority." This is a favorite trick especially of the green movement—as in, "The National Academy of Sciences says that man-made global warming is real so it must be," or, "The Intergovernmental Panel on Climate Change represents the expert views of 2,500 of the world's top scientists: who are you to say they're wrong?" Reply that all it takes is one scientist to falsify a hypothesis: in fact, that's exactly how science is done, with one paradigm replacing another: think Copernicus (or Galileo) and the heliocentric theory of the solar system. Why is it, dear liberal, that you

CONTINUED ON NEXT PAGE

CONTINUED FROM PREVIOUS PAGE

always want to close off debate whether it's about science or anything else in the name of your authorities and political correctness? Is it because liberals believe (as William F. Buckley noted) that everyone has a right to his own opinion—and then are shocked and outraged to find there is another opinion?

Give them another reason why Obama has GOT to go.

NO. 11.

He's a walking foreign policy disaster area. Consider his mission to improve relations with Moscow, sending Hillary Clinton with an oversized prop button that supposedly said "Re-set" in Russian, but which actually said "Overcharge." The result of this diplomatic initiative—which included selling the Poles down the river by removing their anti-ballistic missile shield—was a promise by President Putin to give Venezuela's Hugo Chavez the same nuclear energy capacity and rocket program he had already offered to Iran. Nice work, Barack!

176

Quote the wisdom of
Al "Pinocchio" Gore:

"I think the cost of energy will come down when we make this transition to renewable energy."

Reclaim rock for conservatism:

If John Lennon really found it so easy to "imagine no possessions," how come he had to record his song "Imagine" on a white grand piano in a vast stucco-fronted Georgian mansion on a 72-acre estate in one of the most expensive counties in Britain? Tell your liberal friend you much prefer integrity in your music—take for instance, "The Ballad of the Green Berets" (a number one hit in 1966) sung without a lot of whoop-dee-do by an authentic Green Beret, Barry Sadler.

Conservative history:

Explode another liberal myth: abolitionist "hero" John Brown wasn't one of the good guys, he was a murdering psychopath. At the 1856 Pottawatomie Creek Massacre, he and his fanatical followers dragged five innocent men—none of them slave owners—from their beds and slaughtered them in front of their screaming families. "But like you Stalinists say, you can't make an omelet without breaking eggs, right?"

179

Ask a liberal to guess who came up with this marvelous, well-meaning program:

We ask that the government undertake the obligation above all of providing citizens with adequate opportunity for employment and earning a living. The activities of the individual must not be allowed to clash with the interests of the community, but must take place within its confines and be for the good of all. Therefore, we demand: . . . an end to the power of the financial interests. We demand profit sharing in big business. We demand a broad extension of care for the aged. We demand . . . the greatest possible consideration of small business in the purchases of national, state, and

CONTINUED ON NEXT PAGE

municipal governments. In order to make possible to every capable and industrious [citizen] the attainment of higher education and thus the achievement of a post of leadership, the government must provide an all-around enlargement of our entire system of public education. . . . We demand the education at government expense of gifted children of poor parents. . . . The government must undertake the improvement of public health—by protecting mother and child, by prohibiting child labor. . . by the greatest possible support for all clubs concerned with the physical education of youth. We combat the . . . materialistic spirit within and without us, and are convinced that a permanent recovery of our people can only proceed from within on the foundation of the common good before the individual good.

Yep, it was the Nazi Party, Munich, February 1920.

180

Pick a fight with a liberal on:

. . . .

"SUSTAINABILITY."

Mmm. It sounds so nice, doesn't it? *Sustain*—the word Sting chants (we can imagine) during his interminable tantric yoga sessions. *Sustenance*—stuff that tastes good and keeps you going. *Sustainability*—making sure that never again does the world suffer the mass slaughter of the buffalo or an overfishing disaster. . . . Don't be fooled. The real reason you hear "sustainability" bandied about so much these days is because of a Marxist power grab which began at the 1992 Rio Earth Summit when chief organizer and One World Government advocate Maurice Strong inserted the word into key documents. Since then it has spread like a virus through government and grass roots activist organizations. What "sustainability" really means is giving eco-Nazis over whom you have no democratic control carte blanche to dictate how you use your land, when and how you can travel, and even when you take a shower.

. . . . · 365 WAYS TO DRIVE A LIBERAL CRAZY · . . . .

181

Reclaim rock for conservatism:

. . . .

Quote Frank Zappa: "The United States is a nation of laws, badly written and randomly enforced." Fewer laws equals more freedom—only a liberal could be opposed to that.

182

Start a rumor:

The REAL reason Obama is so sore with the British is that they keep threatening to release the secret intelligence files on his Kenyan grandfather. Turns out during the Mau Mau rebellion he was one of their most successful informants—codenamed MOLERAT. Any abuse or imprisonment he suffered was solely to make his cover story more credible.

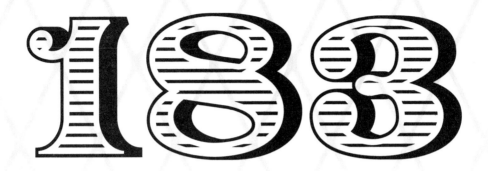

Conservative history:

Torment a liberal with the horrible tale of affirmative action gone oh-so-poetically wrong: *Regents of the University of California* v. *Bakke* (1978). Allan Bakke was a white med school applicant, initially denied a place despite his superior grades because of the University's PC affirmative action program that gave preference to ethnic minorities with much lower grades. One of the five black students admitted to the med school instead of Bakke was Patrick Chavis, whose subsequent "successful" career was compared favorably by affirmative action champions with Bakke's relatively undistinguished one as proof that social justice had been secured. What they neglected to report was Chavis's subsequent suspension by California's medical board for his "inability to perform

CONTINUED ON NEXT PAGE

CONTINUED FROM PREVIOUS PAGE

some of the most basic duties required of a physician." He botched one patient's liposuction, hiding her in his home for forty hours, while she lost 70 percent of her blood; caused another patient severe bleeding, again stashing her in his home; and caused another to suffer a heart attack before bleeding to death.

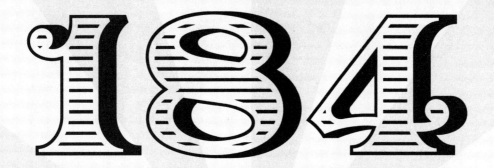

184

To be quoted whenever a liberal tries playing the race card about slavery:

"Blacks were not enslaved because they were black but because they were available. Slavery has existed in the world for thousands of years. Whites enslaved other whites in Europe for centuries before the first black was brought to the Western hemisphere. Asians enslaved Europeans. Asians enslaved other Asians. Africans enslaved other Africans, and indeed even today in North Africa, blacks continue to enslave blacks."—Thomas Sowell

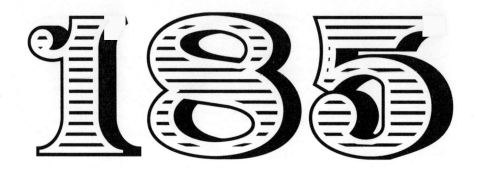

185

Tell a liberal how much you admire the lofty neutrality and commitment to truth at all costs of their house journal the *New York Times*.

· ·

NO. 2.

The *Times* has not endorsed a Republican presidential candidate since Dwight Eisenhower.

186

Start a rumor:

Following the Fort Hood tragedy, the U.S. military decided to extend its "Don't Ask, Don't Tell" policy to Islamist extremists so that never again will they be harassed or embarrassed as poor Major Nidal Malik Hasan was with awkward, unfair, provocative questions like, "Sir, are you sure it's right that a U.S. army officer should be posting on a Jihadist website?" and "Sir, why are you a pointing that gun at me and shouting Allahu Akbar?"

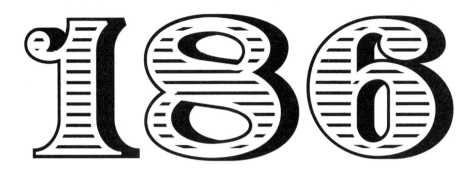

187

Campaign against aid for Africa—which has the opposite effect of the one intended.

Between 1970 and 1998 when well-meaning foreign aid was at its peak, the poverty rate in Africa rose from 11 percent to 66 percent. Why? Because foreign aid end in the hands of corrupt dictators—who are estimated to steal around $10 billion (about half Africa's foreign aid receipts) every year. Argue that what Africans need is "shock therapy," not liberal NGO workers swanning round the country in Land Cruisers. Free trade, property rights, and open markets will do far more than cash handouts. Say you got all this from a book called *Dead Aid* by a black African Harvard masters graduate, Dambisa Moyo.

188

Combat sexism:

List the vast number of sports where women are capable of competing with men on equal terms and winning: Tiddlywinks; curling; free diving; er....

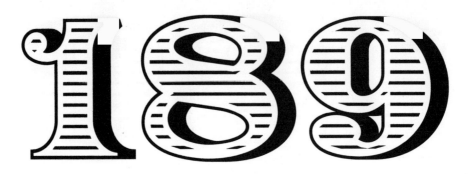

189

Give them another reason why Obama has GOT to go.

NO. 12.

He's unfit to be commander in chief. Say what you like about Dubya posing on the aircraft carrier: at least it reminded people that he'd once been in uniform and showed he cared about the military. But as the infamous *Rolling Stone* interview with General McChrystal revealed, Obama simply isn't interested in military issues and is unprepared to talk in a substantive manner with his commanders. No wonder he had to sack the man who told it like it is.

190

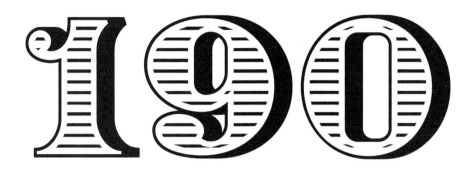

Tell a joke:

Q: What do you get when you offer a liberal a penny for his thoughts?

A: Change.

191

Quote the Reverend Al Sharpton:

"White folks was in caves while we was building empires. We taught them philosophy and astrology and mathematics before Socrates and them Greek homos ever got round to it." Then ask: a) if he's boasting about the Egyptians—presumably he approves of slavery? b) Does he maybe mean astronomy rather than astrology? Or is he really claiming that one of the great historic black achievements is inventing newspaper columns that read, "With Capricorn on the cusp of Leo, expect confusion from a mysterious, dark stranger."

192

Tell a joke:

Q: What's the difference between a liberal and the rear end of a horse?

A: I don't know, either.

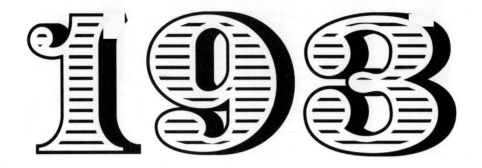

Say:

"My problem with Obama isn't that he's black. My problem with Obama is that he's a white liberal."

194

Teach your kids to read at a young age using the "synthetic phonics" method.

This annoys liberal teachers on so many levels. It will confirm them in their bitter view that middle class kids have an "unfair" advantage. It implies that teaching a child to read is much easier than liberal teachers like to pretend it is. It offends the trendy liberal view that children should be allowed to develop literacy skills as late as possible so that it doesn't interfere with their "creativity."

195

Give your employees
the afternoon off work

to celebrate the anniversary of Ronald Reagan's 1981 sacking of the Air Traffic Controllers, whose union demanded 17 times more than the generous $40 million pay increase it had originally accepted. Explain that you've absolutely no objection to honoring the employee's right to strike—just so long as they don't have any objections to the employer's right to sack.

196

Time to invite your liberal friends 'round for another barbecue.

Why? To celebrate the day when the lives of hundreds of thousands of young American and Allied servicemen were saved thanks to President Truman's fine, principled decision to drop the atom bomb on Hiroshima. Serve Kamikaze cocktails (natch): equal parts Vodka, Triple Sec, and lime juice.

197

Destroy a liberal's argument by exposing the underlying rhetorical cheat.

· ·

NO. 2.

Argumentum ad hominem. "Ad homs"—as they're colloquially known—are one of Johnny Libtard's favorite debating weapons, as in Michael Moore's rant: "I would like to apologize for referring to George W. Bush as a deserter. What I meant to say is that George W. Bush is a deserter, an election thief, a drunk driver, a WMD liar, and a functional illiterate. And he poops his pants."

Liberals like ad homs because, unlike you, they have neither logic nor facts on their side and must therefore resort to personal insults which are the last refuge

CONTINUED ON NEXT PAGE

CONTINUED FROM PREVIOUS PAGE

of a scoundrel. Explain this to a liberal friend—and then call him a stupid libtard. When he accuses you of using *argumentum ad hominem* say: "Hey, I never said ad homs weren't allowed. All I said was that it's kind of tragic when you're so desperate that they're pretty much the only rhetorical weapon you've got."

198

Never speak of "Affirmative Action"—only of "Reverse Discrimination."

Elaborate by saying how angry it makes you that talented blacks, Mexican-Americans, and others who secured their jobs and their college places purely on their own merit will forever be looked on with suspicion and resentment as having gotten there purely because of the color of their skin (or other minority-qualifying attributes).

199

Call your liberal friends to ask why they haven't yet thanked you for your Hiroshima Day celebration barbecue and Kamikaze cocktails.

Was it something you said? Tell them if they like, they can come over for another celebration tonight because it's Nagasaki Day (August 9), anniversary of the second atom bomb which finally led to the surrender of evil, warmongering Imperial Japan. Quote literary historian Paul Fussell on how it felt to hear the news: "We learned to our astonishment that we would not be obliged in a few months to rush up the beaches near Tokyo assault-firing while being machine-gunned, mortared, and shelled, and for all the practiced phlegm of our tough facades we broke down and cried with relief and joy. We were going to live."

200

Start a rumor:

Arnold Schwarzenegger is now the world's fourteenth richest man. He made his fortune by short-selling shares in Californian industries, shortly before introducing his sweeping program of job-destroying, green-bureaucrat-boosting eco-legislation.

201

Pick a fight with a liberal on:

MEN AND WOMEN ARE DIFFERENT.

(No, really.) Ask if God really meant women to have careers as long, hard-working, and well-paid as men's, how come he gave them wombs, breasts, and nurturing instincts?

202

Global Warming Fun.

NO. 8.

On a bright August day at an outdoor gathering where liberals are present, raise your glass to the sky, then shake your head sadly. Announce: "Sheesh! I'm gonna miss this stuff. You really sure I can't change your mind?" When asked about what, say: "You know. *This*. Nice weather. The thing you guys want to ban."

203

Tell a joke:

Q: Why do so many liberals live in LA?

A: It's the only city easy enough for them to spell.

204

Quote Joe Biden, spelling bee champion:

"Look, [John's McCain's] last-minute economic plan does nothing to tackle the number-one job facing the middle class, and it happens to be, as Barack says, a three-letter word: jobs. J-O-B-S, jobs."

Reclaim rock for conservatism:

Refuse to accept that Bruce Springsteen's "Born in the USA" is anything other than a Great Conservative Rock Song—a masterpiece of tub-thumping, gung-ho, redneck patriotism. If mention is made of the anti-war sentiments in the verses about blue collar victims of Vietnam, simply go, "Yeah whatever. No one listens to those bits anyway." Then confirm your point by singing, "Born in the USA! Born in the USA! Born in the USA!" really loudly.

206

Refer to Obama's energy czar Dr. Steven Chu

. . . .

as "the Tin Foil Hat guy" or the "Santorini guy" after his brilliant scheme—proposed at a 2008 London climate change conference—to paint all our rooftops and sidewalks white, in a kind of Greek Island style. Apparently the energy saved would be the equivalent of taking all cars off the road for eleven years. Suggest that maybe next he'll want to be examining the potential of mining the moon for green cheese or extracting sunbeams from cucumbers.

207

On August 17, 1945, George Orwell's *Animal Farm* was published.

It's so easy to read, even liberals can understand it. Donate two dozen or so copies to your kids' class. Make sure to underline the passage where Orwell encapsulates the hypocrisy of the liberal notion of social justice: "All animals are equal. But some animals are more equal than others."

208

Reclaim rock for conservatism:

Marvel at the hypocrisy and stupidity of rock stars, as evidenced by the Beatles song "Taxman." Despite articulating clearly and sensibly the horrors of living under a socialist government where the top rate of tax was 95 percent, they still refused to consider voting conservative.

Quote the wisdom of
Al "Boy Scout" Gore:

"We are ready for any unforeseen event that may or may not occur."

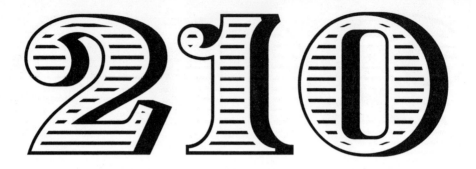

210

Pretend not to understand the phrase, "It's all about oil."

Say, "What possible better motive for military action could there be than to guarantee secure American access to the most vital commodity in the world?"

211

Tutor a liberal's kids in the ways of conservative righteousness—Lesson 2.

Make them watch *The Lion, the Witch and the Wardrobe*. Liberals disapprove of this film because the Christian allegory is so overt. So that's one good reason to show it to their kids. Explain that the White Witch is probably modeled on Obama's enviro czar Carol Browner and that the world where it's "always winter but never Christmas" is a realistic projection of how the United States will look once global cooling kicks in and no one will be able to afford to heat their homes because of carbon taxes introduced to prevent "global warming."

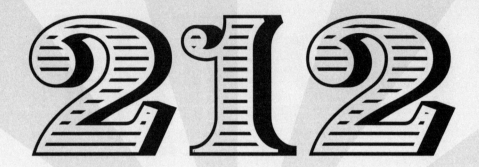

212

Tell a joke:

Q: What's the difference between Obama's cabinet and a penitentiary?

A: One is filled with blackmailers, tax-evaders, and threats to society. The other's for housing prisoners.

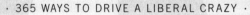

213

Invite your liberal friends to a Norman Borlaug birthday dinner celebration.

Give them two dining options: organic or Borlaug. Treat those who opt for "organic" to a small, misshapen carrot, explaining apologetically that that's all you can spare because organic food is so costly and land-expensive. Treat those who take the Borlaug option to as much genetically modified food as they can possibly eat—true to the spirit of the great American agronomist who saved perhaps a billion lives by launching his "green revolution" using genetically modified strains of wheat, which rescued countries like India and Pakistan from starvation.

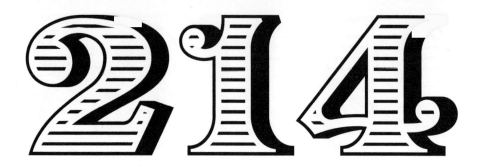

214

Quote Joe Biden, economist,

"People look at me and say, 'What are you talking about, Joe? You're telling me we've got to go spend money to keep from going bankrupt?' The answer is, 'Yes, I'm telling ya.'"

Conservative history:
Defend the Vietnam War.

Point out to any handy liberal that the United States *won* the Vietnam War. America was never defeated on the battlefield, after all, and the United States compelled North Vietnam to sign a peace treaty. When American troops left South Vietnam, it was still a sovereign, independent, non-Communist country, and American troops had also given the rest of East Asia a 2 1/2-year breathing space from Communist expansion. It was only after the liberal Democrat Congress refused to hold North Vietnam accountable for violating the peace accords and walked away from America's commitment to South Vietnam that victory became defeat. The lesson: liberals can't be trusted—by us or by our allies.

216

Conservative terminology.

Whenever discussing Man-Made Global Warming, always refer to it as "Man-BearPig," after the ludicrous imaginary monster invented by Al Gore in a famous episode of *South Park*.

Ask them to guess who said this:

"The soundest way to raise revenues in the long run is to cut taxes now. The purpose of cutting taxes now is … to achieve the more prosperous, expanding economy which can bring a budget surplus." Ronald Reagan? One of the Bushes? F. A. Hayek? Arthur Laffer?

No: JFK.

Conservative party piece:

On being served Fair Trade coffee, take a sip, then spit it out in horror and disgust. Gag: "My God! This is *Fair Trade*! Don't you know I *never* do Fair Trade stuff? Fair Trade is *evil*." Explain the reason for your principled objection: by overpaying certain favored suppliers, Fair Trade sends out incorrect price signals that distort the market. If coffee prices are low, it's not a sign that well-meaning liberals should be emotionally blackmailed into paying more; it's a sign of oversupply which—were the market allowed to work correctly—would send a signal to farmers to diversify their portfolio of crops.

219

Wonder aloud to your liberal friends:

Why was it okay for Obama to accept more than a million inflation-adjusted dollars from Goldman Sachs employees if it was wrong, as liberals protested at the time, for George W. Bush to accept less than one-seventh as much (less than 150,000-inflation adjusted dollars) from Enron? Then wonder aloud at the brilliance of Goldman Sachs—investing in its own bailout and (with donations to the man sure to take his place) buying top-notch jobs in the Obama administration for a discount price.

220

Tell a liberal how much you admire the lofty neutrality and commitment to truth at all costs of their house journal the *New York Times*.

NO. 3.

The *Times* gloatingly, cheerleadingly reported the case of the Duke lacrosse players who had supposedly raped a Durham stripper—(a liberal dream story: rich white kids gang rape a poor black woman)—right up until the point where it emerged that the boys might be innocent. When a *Times* reporter tried writing a story summarizing the defense lawyer's evidence, the story was killed and the

CONTINUED ON NEXT PAGE

reporter replaced with someone more sympathetic to the prosecution. The *Times* also kept standing up for DA Mike Nifong—until his handling of the case was shown to be so corrupt he was disbarred and sent to jail. After a public outcry from disgusted readers, the *Times* claimed that "most flaws flowed from journalistic lapses rather than ideological bias." Uh-huh.

221

Start a new fashion chain

specializing in tacky urban street wear, made in sweatshops by crippled children in Southeast Asia. Make sure the name of your company logo is brandished in very bold letters on all products: OPRAH, INC.

222

Quote Margaret Thatcher:

"The problem with socialism is that eventually you run out of other people's money."

Ask:

If the Obama administration isn't socialist, how come Americans had to pay more to the government in taxes in 2010 than they spent on food, clothing, and shelter combined?

224

Start a rumor:

Just as Woody Allen would never miss his Monday evening slot playing New Orleans jazz clarinet at Manhattan's Carlyle Hotel, so Supreme Court Justice Elena Kagan refuses to let the dignity of her judicial robes interfere with her regular Saturday night appearance as a female mud-wrestler fighting under her *nom-de-guerre* Ivana Slipalot at the Happy Girlzzz Bar in Soho.

225

Pick a fight with a liberal on:

EQUALITY.

Tell that them that, like all meritocrats, you're fine with people making the most of their opportunities, but you're adamantly opposed to "equality of outcome," and you know that "equality of opportunity" has become a liberal bait and switch justifying all sorts of affirmative action-type schemes. Equality under the law is good, equality under the eyes of God is a fact, but any other artificial imposition of "equality" is another word for tyranny. Such egalitarianism was tried and failed miserably and bloodily in Stalin's Soviet Union and Mao's China, so why is Obama so keen to introduce it here?

Tutor a liberal's kids in the ways of conservative righteousness—Lesson 3.

Make them watch *The Lord of the Rings* trilogy. Afterwards, over burgers and fries, invite them to identify the modern parallels. They're probably too young to appreciate—as National Review Online correctly identified in its Best Conservative Movies series—that Wormtongue was clearly modeled on Keith Olbermann. But with a bit of prodding they should recognize the Orcs versus the Shire confrontation as the Clash of Civilizations between militant Islam and the West. Or, alternatively, between the evil Obama administration and the forces of conservative decency, wisdom, and justice.

227

Quote the wisdom of Al "All-American" Gore.

"Who are these people?" (To a tour guide at Monticello after seeing busts of George Washington and Ben Franklin.)

228

Global Warming Fun.

NO. 9.

At the first hint of a fall chill, run around in terror near your liberal friends, tearing at your hair and shouting "Aiieeee! Aiiieee! It comes, it comes. The great ice age comes!" Then apologize, slap your forehead, and say: "Wait. My mistake. The ice age was the thing all your gurus were predicting in the 1970s. You've changed your minds now, right? All this increasingly cold weather we're getting—it's a sign of, er, *global warming*, yeah?"

229

Pick a fight with a liberal on:

GREAT PRESIDENTS.

How come libtard sleazebuckets like JFK and meddling early socialists like Woodrow Wilson and FDR tend to figure so high in the list of great presidents? The truly great presidents are the ones who interfered as little as possible, leaving America's natural capitalist instincts free to pursue prosperity and liberty. It's presidents like Republicans Warren Harding (who got the United States swiftly out of a post-World War I depression) and Calvin Coolidge we should really celebrate: on their watch taxes fell, wages increased, working hours declined, and the United States enjoyed one of its greatest-ever booms. FDR, on the other hand, just made the Great Depression worse.

230

Destroy a liberal's argument by exposing the underlying rhetorical cheat.

· ·

NO. 3.

The motive fallacy. This is a common technique used by liberals to dismiss facts that don't suit their argument. For example: "Well I'm not going to believe anything X says about this. X is funded by Exxon." Simply point out that just because somebody has a reason to believe something doesn't necessarily mean what he believes is not true. As philosopher Jamie Whyte puts it: "A man may stand to gain a great deal of peace and quiet from telling his wife that he loves her. But he really may love her nevertheless."

231

Start a rumor:

Robert Redford always vowed that he would never have plastic surgery. That's because, concealed beneath the mole on his cheek was the homing device which allowed his KGB paymasters to track their most illustrious agent at all times. However, in 2002, disappointed by the right-ward drift Russia was taking, he decided to sever his links with his former ideological soul mate—and had the mole transmitter removed.

232

Pick a fight with a liberal on:

ELITISM.

Liberals believe in egalitarianism. They don't often get called on it, though, because no one bothers to defend elitism—but you should. Ask a liberal, "So you really disapprove of competition and hierarchy and achievement and want everything to be equal do you? Well, answer me this, if you were president and you needed a handful of troops to do a delicate, dangerous job, who would you turn to—a unit of racially and sexually and disability diverse troops or the elite: Special Forces, Navy Seals, Delta Force? When you watch football, assuming you're willing to watch something so violent and competitive, do you want to watch the elite, the best of the best, the professionals who made it to the NFL

CONTINUED ON NEXT PAGE

CONTINUED FROM PREVIOUS PAGE

on the basis of their talent and training, or a United Nations-coordinated rainbow coalition of teams drawn from men and women from around the world to make it a truly global unisex game? Or suppose you needed serious surgery, would you prefer the operation to be done by a surgeon with years of practice behind him, drawn from the elite of the medical profession, or by a deserving recent immigrant, selected for the task as a result of the new Obamafair™ social justice program designed to boost the self-esteem of low-skill workers while simultaneously combating society's sexist, racist, elitist hegemony?"

Stage a demonstration outside your local branch of Whole Foods.

Protest that organic is an oppressive, quasi-racist, middle-class fad that exhausts vast acreages that could be put to much better use growing the kind of intensive, genetically modified crops that we need to feed the world—or is that the point: you really don't want to feed the world because you think Mother Earth needs fewer children?

234

Tell a joke:

Q: Why won't Obama release his birth certificate?

A: The ink isn't dry yet.

235

Start a rumor:

Janet Napolitano's Department of Homeland Security has decided to revise its color code warning system.

If a small-scale terrorist attack—fewer than 100 expected dead—is imminent, Ms. Napolitano will describe the situation as "calm"—Color Code: Turquoise

If a larger scale terrorist attack—in the league of 9/11—is imminent, Ms. Napolitano will describe the situation as "relaxed"—Color Code: Ecru.

If Al Qaeda is about to destroy New York and Los Angeles simultaneously with a selection of strategically positioned nuclear devices, like in *24* only way worse—Ms. Napolitano will describe the situation as "vibrant"—Color Code: Taupe.

All of this is intended to show the Muslim world that the Obama administration will not "overreact" to terrorism the way the bad old Bush administration did.

236

Tell a liberal how much you appreciate that the Obama economy is a system of checks and balances.

· ·

He writes the checks, you pay the balance.

Conservative party trick:

Next time you're out drinking with a liberal—presuming you can bear to do such a thing—casually reach for his wallet and help yourself to a few bucks. When he complains, look at him in puzzlement: "But surely you don't believe in *property*, do you? Anyway, I'm just spreading the wealth around."

238

Buy a roulette set. Invite your liberal friends over for a "fun" version of the game especially adapted to their ideological enthusiasms.

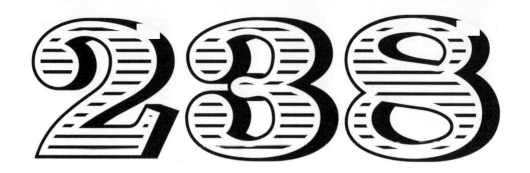

When they lose, you—the bank (that is, the government)—take all their chips. But whenever they win, temper their delight by paying out only 60 percent of the proceeds. Divide the remaining 40 percent among the other players. Smile brightly: "So much friendlier this way, don't you think, when everything is shared equally?"

You're Invited!

Pick a fight with a liberal on:

SOCIAL STIGMA.

Liberals are forever congratulating themselves on having all but eliminated the "stifling" codes of disapproval by which the pre-1960s generations dictated socially acceptable norms. But "stigma" was good. While stigma existed, poor people were too proud to beg or rely on welfare; girls were too ashamed to be thought "loose" or to seek single motherhood as a lifestyle choice; men were more chivalrous because there was a stigma against treating women without deference and special consideration; and people were more polite and even dressed properly as a sign of respect for others and themselves. "Stigma" was the means by which free citizens could agree on a mutually satisfactory code of

CONTINUED ON NEXT PAGE

CONTINUED FROM PREVIOUS PAGE

behavior, without the agents of the state having to poke their noses into anyone's private business. Liberals, however, utterly reverse the equation—they're all for obliterating taboos, knocking down stigmas, shocking the middle class, and preaching tolerance for the most anti-social behavior; and then they turn around and act as the biggest advocates of *the government* dictating private behavior with the nanny state. The consequences? Greater government intrusion; much worse behavior.

240

Conservative history:
Stand up for Joe McCarthy.

PART 1.

Point out that, if anything, he underestimated the extent of Soviet infiltration in the U.S. government and that virtually all the people he called before the congressional committees were involved in networks controlled by the Kremlin.

241

Stand up for Joe McCarthy.

· ·

PART 2.

Buy a copy of Ann Coulter's book *Treason* and give it to a liberal friend, with the inscription, "Hey, guess what: Communist infiltration of the government didn't begin with Obama after all!"

242

Tell a joke:

Q: How do you starve an Obama supporter?

A: Hide his food stamps under his work boots.

243

Praise the "Burqa" as a truly great symbol of female liberation.

Say you've always respected the notion that it's a woman's inalienable right to go out in public dressed like a tent.

244

Tell a joke:

Q: Why did God give liberals annoying, whiny voices?

A: So that even the blind could hate them.

245

Affect puzzlement at the curious fact that the 2002 Beltway sniper murders were initially blamed by investigators on an "angry white man."

Then wonder why, after the perpetrators were discovered to be inconveniently black and Muslim, the liberal media persistently referred to killer John Muhammad by his pre-conversion name John Williams; and why authorities chose to play down the possibility that the cold blooded assassination of ten Americans by two Islamic converts rambling about jihad had anything to do with terrorism or the "Religion of Peace."

Diss a liberal movie:

Deconstruct the subtext of *Brokeback Mountain* as an example of liberal fascism, as noted by Jonah Goldberg: "Two perfect male specimens are at home only in the pastoral wild, away from the bourgeois conventions of modern life. At home in nature, they are finally free to give themselves over to their instinctual desires. But they cannot live in the hills, indulging their instincts. So they spend the rest of their lives trapped in soul-crippling traditional marriages, their only joy their annual 'fishing trips,' where they try to re-create the ecstasy of their authentic encounter...." Yep. Hermann Goering and Joseph Goebbels would definitely have given this Nazi soft-porn masterpiece a double thumbs up.

247

Quote Ludwig von Mises:

. . . .

"Whoever prefers life to death, happiness to suffering, well-being to misery must defend without compromise private ownership in the means of production."

248

Give them another reason why Obama has GOT to go.

. . . .

NO. 13.

He can't bear the idea that the United States is a superpower, as he showed when he said at a Washington Nuclear Security Summit: "It is a vital national security interest of the United States to reduce these conflicts because whether we like it or not, we remain a dominant military superpower, and when conflicts break out, one way or another we get pulled into them. And that ends up costing us significantly in terms of both blood and treasure." Maybe he'd feel more comfortable running somewhere less superpowery, like maybe Swaziland or Papua, New Guinea? If he did, there are plenty of us out here who would give him our fullest support.

249

As winter approaches, keep *Human Events*'s "Ten Most Dangerous Books of the 19th and 20th Century" in a pile by your fire or stove:

The Communist Manifesto; Mein Kampf; Quotations from Chairman Mao; The Kinsey Report; Das Kapital; Betty Friedan's *The Feminine Mystique;* Comte's *The Course of Positive Philosophy;* Nietzsche's *Beyond Good and Evil;* Keynes's *General Theory of Employment, Interest and Money.* When a liberal asks what they're doing there, reply: "Kindling."

250

Rail against the iniquities of government-to-government "foreign aid."

Quote the definition of economist Peter Bauer. It is a transfer "from the poor in rich countries to the rich in poor countries."

251

When employing the word "progressive," always use air quotes.

Explain to a liberal that you cannot fathom what is remotely "progressive" about the kind of ideology which seeks to reduce U.S. per capita income to levels last seen in the 1860s.

252

Start a rumor:

The radical, fringy, and racially incendiary Reverend Jeremiah Wright was actually Barack Obama's pastor and friend for two decades—oh wait, that's true!

Conservative party game:

Liberals always like to consider themselves bastions of tolerance. So push the boundaries with this little game, as personally tested with enormous success by your author. Buy your kids a pack of those realistic fake cigarettes which puff out dust at the end so it looks like your kid is really smoking. Tell them not to be too obvious about it, but next time you find yourself at a social engagement where kids mix with grown ups, get them to wander around "smoking" nonchalantly as if it's something they do all the time. For maximum impact, you could even have them come up to you and say, "Dad/Mom. You got a cigarette?" "Sure son," you can reply, retrieving a fake cigarette from a real pack and "lighting" it for them. The important thing is to make absolutely no comment and act as if this is all the most normal behavior in the world. Relish the liberals' tension and discomfort as they agonize over how best to confront you over your disgracefully lax parenting. It really is about as fun as fun gets.

254

Pick a fight with a liberal on:

FAIRNESS.

The top 5 percent of taxpayers contribute 60 percent of government revenue; the top 10 percent of taxpayers contribute 75 percent of revenue; another two-fifths make up the rest. Half the U.S. population is now exempt from paying tax. 2012 may turn out to be the first presidential election in American history where non-taxpaying voters outnumber taxpaying voters. At this point, remind the liberal: "Still, I guess the imbalance will find a way of working itself out in the end. Your side thinks it can go on taking more and more of our money. Our side has most of the guns and ammunition."

255

Quote from the collected wisdom of Al "Non Sequitur" Gore:

"I am not part of the problem. I am a Democrat."

Define multiculturalism:

State-sanctioned grievance industry that stokes division and resentment, while always under the delusion that it is doing something positive called "celebrating diversity."

257

Force them to sit down with a beer and watch *Starship Troopers* (1997).

This is perhaps the greatest 'Nam movie ever made because it's one of the few (John Wayne's *Green Berets* and the Mel Gibson flick *We Were Soldiers* get honorable mention here) that doesn't say America is bad or ask you to feel guilty. On the contrary, it invites you to rejoice in the death of America's enemies, and to cheer their annihilation in any number of gruesome and satisfying ways. That's because in this 'Nam parable, the VC and NVA are played by evil, insectoid-alien hell creatures.

258

Tell a joke:

Q. What's the difference between Obamacare and a car battery?

A. The car battery has a positive side.

259

On Columbus Day, loudly express your gratitude that America was taken away from backward, cruel, and bloodthirsty Indian tribes and given over to Christian European civilization.

. . . .

Go further and tell your liberal friends that you've always admired how Cortez and his small band of men conquered the Aztec empire, abolishing a culture based on human sacrifice. As they stand there spluttering, you can rub it in: "You have a problem with that?"

260

Praise the marvelous "inclusivity" and "diversity" of the United Nations Human Rights Council,

whose membership includes such bastions of free speech, fair play, and democracy as Cuba, Saudi Arabia, China, and Burkina Faso. Praise also the great sense of humor the organization has demonstrated in the past, like the time in 2002 when—under its old name the United Nations Human Rights Commission—forty of its members (including Zimbabwe and Sudan) passed a resolution affirming the "right" of the Palestinians to fight Israel by "all available means including armed struggle."

261

Say to a liberal, "You remember the Reagan era, when Ronald Reagan was President, and Bob Hope and Johnny Cash were still with us?

· ·

Well, now we have Obama, no hope, and no cash."

262

Throw a party

. . . .

to celebrate the fact that each passing day brings us closer to knowing which Republican candidate has defeated Obama by a landslide. You might even keep a giant tear-off-a-sheet calendar on your front lawn, marking each day as a "Countdown to the end of the Obama administration."

263

Campaign for the eradication of the California delta smelt.

This small, dumb, pointless, silvery fish, the twenty-first century snail darter, is devastating the lives of farmers in the San Joaquin valley and sending California's economy even further down the drain. Because of federal eco-protection laws, farmers have been forbidden from irrigating their parched crops lest the precious delta smelt's breeding grounds be compromised. A protest sign, "Save the Farmers!" will leave liberals conflicted because they're wedded to the idea that they're pro-farmer (though they're not really). You could also end the whole controversy by starting a delta smelt hatchery and selling the otherwise unproductive fish as fish bait.

264

Reclaim rock for conservatism:

Dispute the premise of Edwin Starr's "War—What Is It Good For?" Answer the seemingly rhetorical question, "Quite a lot actually—it's been used to defend liberty, save Jews from extermination, prevent Nazis from running Europe, free blacks from slavery—you know, little things like that."

265

Tell a liberal how much you admire the lofty neutrality and commitment to truth at all costs of their house journal the *New York Times.*

NO. 4.

Congratulate them on the paper's brave, innovative, and imaginative experiment to merge total fiction with conventional factual news reportage by employing fabulist Jayson Blair. Say how disgusted you were by the obviously racist rumor that the only reason the *Times* kept the guy on for four years and employed him to write 600 articles was because of the color of his skin. Add: "Anyway, even if that WAS the reason, I agree with Arthur Sulzberger Jr.: It's SO much more important that a newspaper of record puts DIVERSITY before all that old-fashioned crap like factual accuracy."

266

Demand stridently that imperialist Western forces of occupation be withdrawn immediately from all the world's trouble spots and replaced at once by UN "blue helmet" peacekeepers.

Say: "After what those blue helmets achieved preventing those 8,000 Serbs being massacred at Srebrenica and the million Hutus and Tutsis being slaughtered in Rwanda, just imagine what wonders they could work in Afghanistan and Iraq!"

267

Start a rumor:

President Obama is indeed a Manchurian Candidate—but not in the way you might think. In June 1999, a shadowy cabal of right-wing business interests found themselves feeling so utterly nauseated by the Clinton regime that they devised a plan to ensure that by 2012, no Democrat candidate would ever be elected president again. First they needed a Manchurian Candidate: someone so hatefully left-wing and disgracefully incompetent that he would bring the American economy to its knees, while rendering it an international laughing stock. In this way "liberal values" would be tarnished forever in the eyes of American voters. So far, the plan is working brilliantly.

Ask:

. . . .

"If God really cares about cruelty to animals, how come he made foie gras taste so delicious?"

Start a rumor:

Jane Fonda visited Hanoi in 1972 at the instigation of her secret lover Richard Nixon. (Roger Vadim had given her a taste for tall, dark, strange men.) Her mission was to pose as a dumb, treacherous, liberal, anti-Vietnam protestor, lull the Commies into a false sense of security with her breasts and coquettish manner, and sneak homing beacons onto NVA anti-aircraft gun emplacements—all of which were subsequently destroyed on B-52 bombing raids ordered by her secret lover. She also smuggled back messages from downed U.S. pilots, concealing them in a body cavity not likely to be searched by the North Vietnamese. Unfortunately, the letters gave her a painful infection, as did her affair with Nixon, which is the source of Hanoi Jane's lifelong resentment of American prisoners of war. This explains her infamous statement that returning POWs who claimed to have been tortured and brainwashed were "hypocrites and liars." That wasn't the real, kind, generous Jane talking; it was the poxy jilted lover.

270

Ask how come, if liberals are so keen on equality and fairness, they're so much more money-grubbing than conservatives.

According to both the World Values Survey and the General Social Survey, left-wingers are more likely to rate "high income" as an important factor in choosing a job, more likely to say "after good health, money is the most important thing," and agree with the statement "there are no right or wrong ways to make money." This was confirmed by Doug Urbanski, former business manager of libtard documentary-maker Michael Moore, who said: "He is more money-obsessed than anyone I have known—and that's saying a lot."

271

Reclaim rock for conservatism:

Explain to a liberal how James Brown's "It's a Man's World" is the definitive take-down of Mary Wollstonecraft, Simone de Beauvoir, Betty Friedan, Gloria Steinem, and Germaine Greer.

Pick a fight with a liberal on:

. . . .

PC.

PC costs American lives. In 2000 when the USS *Cole* refueled in Yemen's port of Aden, Navy brass were so concerned about appearing to be "sensitive guests" that sailors patrolling the deck were not permitted to carry loaded weapons. Nor did the destroyer deploy "picket boats" and establish a defensive perimeter—even though Yemen had only recently been taken off the State Department's list of countries that sponsored terrorism. All this pandering to imaginary foreign sensitivities made it pitifully easy for an al Qaeda motorized skiff packed with explosives to approach the destroyer and blow a hole in its side, killing seventeen

CONTINUED ON NEXT PAGE

CONTINUED FROM PREVIOUS PAGE

sailors. Two hours after this entirely avoidable terrorist attack, another motorized skiff approached the stricken vessel. A sentry raised his rifle, only to be told by his superior: "Let me tell you something about the rules of engagement. You can't point a loaded weapon at these people. That's an act of aggression." And you wonder why our enemies no longer take U.S. military power seriously?

Quote John Adams on his birthday (October 30):

"All good government is and must be republican." Or, if you prefer, with special application to the Obama administration and the current Supreme Court: "The jaws of power are always open to devour, and her arm is always stretched out, if possible, to destroy the freedom of thinking, speaking, and writing."

On Halloween,

help your kids make Carol Browner and Al Gore horror masks—on unbleached, recycled, Fair Trade paper, obviously—then encourage them to go 'round bugging the hell out of your liberal neighbors by shaking a begging bowl and yelling: "Cap 'n trade! Cap 'n trade!"

275

Enthuse about 9/11 conspiracy theories, the wackier the better.

You'll be preaching to the choir here: in a May 2007 Rasmussen poll, 35 percent of Democrats said they believe George W. Bush had advance knowledge of the attack, while another 26 percent said they're not sure. Say if it wasn't personally ordered by George Bush or Mossad, then it was almost certainly the Illuminati or the lizard-headed master-race known as the Babylonian Brotherhood, whose membership includes George W. Bush, the Queen of England, Kris Kristofferson, and Boxcar Willie.

Explain sincerely how it was you realized the "official version" of 9/11 couldn't possibly be correct: "Well Islam, right, it's a peaceful religion. No way would these devout guys get on a plane and blow innocent people up. Where's the motive? It's not like Muslims have a track record of major international terrorism. . . ."

276

Quote Thomas Sowell:

. . . .

"Socialism in general has a record of failure so blatant that only an intellectual could ignore or evade it."

Politely inquire of liberals just how they're proposing to "Free Tibet"

given that China has an army of around 7.5 million soldiers, none of whom is likely to be impressed by the ramblings of a capitalist running dog lackey like Richard Gere, let alone a few bumper stickers.

278

Make them take the Gore versus Unabomber test.

Simply take random extracts from Al Gore's *Earth in the Balance* and the Unabomber's *Manifesto*—and invite them to guess who wrote what.

279

Ask why it is that liberals have such a problem with civil rights and people of color.

Republicans—founded as the anti-slavery party.

Democrats—wanted to keep blacks in slavery; passed the discriminatory Black Codes and Jim Crow laws; started the Ku Klux Klan.

William Wilberforce (the Briton who campaigned for the abolition of slavery)—a Tory (conservative) Member of Parliament.

280

Play along with the increasingly common liberal habit of equating Israel with Nazi Germany.

Say: "You know what? I think Israel's WAY worse!" Proceed to compare Gaza unfavorably with the Warsaw ghetto; liken the West Bank barrier to the Siegfried Line; accuse the Israeli Defense Force of being even worse than Hitler's Das Reich Panzer Division; claim that Sabra and Chatila were worse than Auschwitz and Treblinka combined. Work yourself up into a lather of rage and indignation. Then say: "I'm sorry. Forgive me for saying this, but you and I both know this in our hearts to be true: there will never be peace and harmony on this planet of ours till the world is *JUDENFREI!*"

281

Start a rumor:

Senator Harry Reid likes to describe his conservative opponents as "evil"—which is a bit rich given his dark, intimate secret. Harry Reid was born with the mark of the beast—666—clearly visible on his left testicle, much to the embarrassment of his devoutly Christian parents. His friend David Seltzer got to hear about this and used the future senator as his model for the evil Damien Anti-Christ child in his spooky 1976 chiller *The Omen*. But to spare the public's blushes, he decided to relocate the Satanic birthmark to the boy's scalp.

282

Pick a fight with a liberal on:

RACE.

Rail against the Great White Liberal Death Wish. What exactly is so hateful and wrong about the white Judeo-Christian culture which created: the Sistine Chapel; the complete works of Shakespeare; the theory of relativity; the computer; the automobile; the Goldberg variations; the American Constitution? Right. So isn't it about time those self-hating white liberals out there, who think we should feel guilty about our achievements, drop our cultural standards, and celebrate "the other," either kept quiet or put their money where their mouth is and moved to one of those places whose vibrancy they so admire. The Congo, maybe; or Somalia; or Turkmenistan.

283

Quote the wisdom of Al Gore:

"Democrats understand the importance of bondage between a mother and child."

Conservative history:

Never let liberals forget that the sub-prime mortgage disaster was Bill Clinton's fault. In 1995 President Clinton's changes to the Community Reinvestment Act enabled ACORN to run a politically correct extortion campaign against mortgage lenders, compelling them by force of law to make unsound (sub-prime) loans to poor minorities who never stood a hope of repaying them.

285

Praise *Ferris Bueller's Day Off* (1986) as perhaps the only intelligent teen comedy liberal Hollywood has ever produced.

Not only does it have a cool, likeable, conservative hero (Matthew Broderick) who bunks off school to avoid liberal indoctrination ("I'm not European. I don't plan on being European. So who gives a crap if they're socialists")—but it even includes a brief explanation of the Smoot-Hawley Tariff Act, the Laffer Curve, and supply-side economics, poignantly delivered by former Nixon aide Ben Stein.

Destroy a liberal's argument by exposing the underlying rhetorical cheat.

NO. 4.

"Closing Down the Argument." In a debate based on fact, a conservative will always win. A sure-fire sign that a liberal is losing is when he tries to "close down the argument" by casting aspersions on your morality. For example, if you are debating immigration, he will accuse you of being a "racist"; if you're worried about radical Islam, you're "Islamophobic"; if you want your kids to be taught properly at school, you're an "elitist"; if you think marriage requires one man and one woman, you're "homophobic;" if you think there are rather obvious dif-

CONTINUED ON NEXT PAGE

CONTINUED FROM PREVIOUS PAGE

ferences between men and women, you're a "sexist"; and so on. This technique says: "My opponent is so satanically evil that what little truth he has to utter is irredeemably tainted by his depravity. Whereas, I'm good and nice and caring, so I win." All you have to do to counter this technique is to point out to the liberal exactly what he's doing.

287

Joke time:

A biker is riding by the zoo, when he sees a little girl leaning into the lion's cage. Suddenly, the lion grabs her by the cuff of her jacket and tries to pull her inside to slaughter her before the eyes of her screaming parents.

The biker jumps off his bike, runs to the cage, and hits the lion square on the nose with a powerful punch. Whimpering from the pain, the lion jumps back, letting go of the girl, and the biker brings her to her terrified parents, who thank him endlessly.

A *New York Times* reporter has witnessed the whole scene, and addressing the biker, says, "Sir, this was the most gallant and brave thing I saw a man do in my whole life."

CONTINUED ON NEXT PAGE

CONTINUED FROM PREVIOUS PAGE

"Why, it was nothing, really, the lion was behind bars. I just saw this little kid in danger, and acted as I felt right."

"Well, I'll make sure this won't go unnoticed. I'm a journalist from the *New York Times*, you know, and tomorrow's paper will have this on the front page. What motorcycle do you ride and what political affiliation do you have?"

"A Harley Davidson, and I am a Republican."

The journalist leaves.

The following morning the biker buys the *New York Times* and reads, on the front page:

REPUBLICAN BIKER GANG MEMBER ASSAULTS AFRICAN IMMIGRANT AND STEALS HIS LUNCH

288

Express profound bafflement over a liberal's positions on abortion and capital punishment.

"So let me get this right: you're in favor of saving the lives of convicted murderers and terrorists? But you're in favor of killing kids who haven't gotten around to doing anything wrong yet and who might turn out nice? Interesting!"

Explode another liberal myth:

Mock the notion that Saladin was any less cruel or more civilized than his Christian opponents. Recall how he treated Crusaders captured at Hattin on July 4, 1187, when Saladin ordered that they should all be beheaded—in accordance with the Koran—and watched, "his face joyful," while his followers slaughtered the infidels.

Reclaim rock for conservatism:

Serenade them with Metallica's "Don't Tread on Me":

> Liberty or death, what we so proudly hail
> once you provoke her, rattling of her tail
> never begins it, never, but once engaged...
> never surrenders, showing the fangs of rage...

Yay! Suck on that, socialist oppressor scum!

291

Tell a joke:

Q: What is the difference between liberalism and communism?

A: The Communist admits it.

292

Quote millionaire rabble-rouser Michael Moore:

"The Iraqis who have risen up against the occupation are not 'insurgents' or 'terrorists' or 'The Enemy.' They are the revolution, the Minutemen, and their numbers will grow—and they will win." Wonder whether maybe it's not too late for Moore to go and share his insights and empathy over a friendly decapitation or two somewhere like Fallujah or Al Amara.

293

Wonder aloud why it is that conservatives are so much more generous than liberals.

(According to *Who Really Cares?* by Arthur Brooks, conservatives give at least 30 percent more to charity; other sources put the figure as high as 100 percent.) Decide that liberalism is a hypocrite's religion that, while preaching altruism, encourages its practitioners to outsource their personal obligations to taxpayers and, more effectively, to conservatives who really do practice the altruistic gospel.

294.

Pick a fight with a liberal on:

IQ.

According to some dumbass survey, the mean IQ of adolescents who identify themselves as "very liberal" is 106, but the mean IQ of adolescents who identify as "very conservative" is 95. Yeah, and we know the real reason why that is: most of those "very liberal" adolescents are in fact ultra-smart conservative kids who know that when you're that age the best way to get all the hottest chicks is to pretend you're some kind of tree-embracing, world-saving bunny-hugger.

295

Quote P. J. O'Rourke:

· ·

"The good news is that, according to the Obama administration, the rich will pay for everything. The bad news is that, according to the Obama administration, you're rich."

296

Tell a liberal how much you admire the lofty neutrality and commitment to truth at all costs of their house journal the *New York Times*.

NO. 5.

Praise the Grey Lady for its principled decision in 2005 to expose President Bush's Terrorist Surveillance wiretap program. Of course, there are conservative fools who witter on about stuff like national security, but liberals understand otherwise. Say to your liberal friend that you would rather a thousand innocent New Yorkers were blown to tiny pieces on the subway than live in a country where

CONTINUED ON NEXT PAGE

CONTINUED FROM PREVIOUS PAGE

government attempts to eavesdrop on potentially innocent jihadists; you're so proud that the crusading zeal and moral certitude for which the *New York Times* is so justly renowned has made that possible.

Celebrate the 1995 repeal of the 55 mph federal speed limit

by taking a liberal for an 80 mph spin through Texas and Utah—the highest speeds currently allowed anywhere in the United States, though of course there really should be no limits at all. As the wind blows through your hair, laughingly quote Ralph Nader who said at the time of the repeal, "History will never forgive Congress for this assault on the sanctity of human life." In fact, as Stephen Moore of the Cato Institute demonstrated, the average fatality rate dropped— even in states that raised speed limits. In 1997, there were 66,000 fewer road injuries than in 1995. So in fact it's not speed that kills; it's ignorant safety Nazis like Nader.

298

Blame the BP oil spill on the green movement.

Because BP spent all those millions re-branding itself as "Beyond Petroleum" and trying to "greenwash" its image by buying into renewable energy, it forgot how to run its core business—drilling for the sticky black stuff the world needs far more than it needs solar power or bird-chomping wind farms.

Teach a liberal a little science: the sea is full of microorganisms that eat petroleum (which is leaking from the seabed all the time).

The BP oil spill in the Gulf, which was supposed to have despoiled the region for decades, will likely have little long-term effect on the fishing industry or the

CONTINUED ON NEXT PAGE

CONTINUED FROM PREVIOUS PAGE

ecological health of the region. Yes, the oil spill was a "disaster," but the idea that we would never again be eating Gulf shrimp or oysters or be able to enjoy the region's beaches was pure eco-hysteria and fear-mongering. Liberals, like little bratty children, are very good at screaming and pointing fingers and passing blame ("It's his fault!") or issuing threats (like Obama's joke of an Interior Secretary Ken Salazar saying he was going to keep his boot on the neck of BP—that really helped)—or Obama haplessly asking whose ass he should kick—(ditto); but it's conservatives who generally keep their heads and get on with the job of fixing the problem. All the liberal hypocrites did was cripple the tourist industry along the Gulf Coast—in typical liberal fashion making a "disaster" worse.

Quote Joe Biden
on choosing a president:

"I believe that's a metaphor, a metaphor for what the country is looking for. They're looking for a sleepover with people they like!"

300

Pick a fight with a liberal on:

OVERPOPULATION.

Scratch beneath the surface of a supposedly kindly, caring green liberal and what you often find underneath is a vicious Nazi eugenicist who believes, as the Club of Rome once put it, that "the common enemy of humanity is man." Greens think the teeming, pullulating masses of humankind—especially in the Third World—should be discouraged from breeding. Otherwise, they fear, scarce resources will be depleted and the planet swamped. To put these fears into perspective, quote this man: "Our teeming population is the strongest evidence our numbers are burdensome to the world, which can hardly support us from its natural elements. Our wants grow more and more keen and our complaints

CONTINUED ON NEXT PAGE

CONTINUED FROM PREVIOUS PAGE

more bitter in all mouths, while nature fails in affording us our usual sustenance. In every deed, pestilence and famine and wars have to be regarded as a remedy for nations as the means of pruning the luxuriance of the human race." Paul Ehrlich in 1968? Al Gore last year? Nope. It was Tertullian, a Carthaginian priest in 210 AD when the world population was 250 million. It's now over 6.5 billion. We haven't been swamped yet, and chances are we won't ever be, because liberals forget that human beings can't be measured solely by consumption, but by their ingenuity and creativity, which help us to develop new resources, find new ways to deal with challenges, discover new ways to protect the environment, and, who knows, maybe in centuries to come even colonize space. Oh, yeah, I forgot: liberals hate "colonialism" too.

301

Pick a fight with a liberal on:

IMPERIALISM.

Liberals hate imperialism because in their mind it's all about the big bad West holding its big bad sway over the rest of the world. Liberals are much more comfortable with Western retreat and "multiculturalism" than with Western dominance and triumphalism. But America, Canada, Hong Kong, Singapore, Malaysia, India, and Australia did pretty well out of imperialism, didn't they, inheriting the ideas of English liberty and law, free market economics, representative government, the English language, etc.? And if you think some people wouldn't welcome a return of imperialism, you might take a trip to Zimbabwe and see what the starving folks there have to say.

302

Tell a joke:

Q: What do Vanilla Ice, Eminem, and Barack Obama have in common?

A: They've all made careers pretending to be black men.

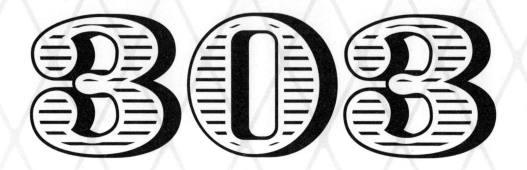

303

Agree that JFK was one of our greatest presidents.

· ·

Suggest this was because he spent less than one term in office, so he never had time to meddle and "improve" things, as liberals are wont to do.

304

Agree that JFK was one of our greatest presidents, part two.

Ask your liberal friend which part of JFK's agenda he liked most: JFK's pledge to increase defense spending to close the "missile gap" with the Soviets, his supply-side tax cuts, his commitment to halt communism in Indochina, or his rousing anti-welfarist line, "Ask not what your country can do for you—ask what you can do for your country."

305

Pick a fight with a liberal on:

LIBERAL DOUBLE STANDARDS.

As Ann Coulter says, funny, isn't it, how liberals want everything they disapprove of banned (smoking, guns, practicing Christianity, ROTC, the Pledge of Allegiance) and whatever they approve of (abortion-on-demand, gay marriage, pornography, condom distribution in public schools, screenings of *An Inconvenient Truth*) made mandatory.

306

List just a few of the things environmental and health advocacy groups would have banned on the "precautionary principle," if only they'd had the chance:

Fire: too hot, hazardous, and burn-y

The wheel: dramatically increased risk of vehicle accidents

Electricity: can cause electrocution; creates obesity in people who sit too long in front of TV sets

CONTINUED ON NEXT PAGE

CONTINUED FROM PREVIOUS PAGE

The internal combustion engine: burns potentially planet-destroying fossil fuels.

The internet: might be used to disseminate dangerous information casting doubts on Man-Made Global Warming and/or pouring scorn/mockery on well-intentioned environmental and health advocacy groups thus impeding their noble battle to make the world entirely safe for everyone.

307

Tell a joke:

An elderly senator, exhausted and ill from enacting Obama's health-care plans, goes to the doctor. Doctor says: "I have bad news, good news, and bad news, Senator. The bad news is that you only have six months to live. But the good news is that there's an operation that is 100 percent successful in curing this illness." "That sounds great. So what's the other bad news?" asks the senator. Replies the doctor: "The Department of Health and Human Services says the first available slot is seven months from today."

308

Tell them they're WRONG.

Liberals hate being told they're wrong: a) because the truth is always painful; and b) because in their warped, liberal world, "right" and "wrong" are alien, almost forbidden concepts. That's why liberals prefer terms like "appropriate" and "inappropriate," because they're non-judgmental. So go ahead. Judge them. Because they're WRONG.

309

Instead of POTUS prefer COOTUS:

. . . .

(Community Organizer of the United States).

310

Start a rumor:

Obama's safe schools czar Kevin Jennings is a reigning champion in the Super Gay Man Olympics. Unfortunately, his two specialist competition categories cannot be detailed here. However, if you want to hear all, just turn up at any of the free Gay, Lesbian, Straight Education Network outreach programs coming soon to a kindergarten class near you.

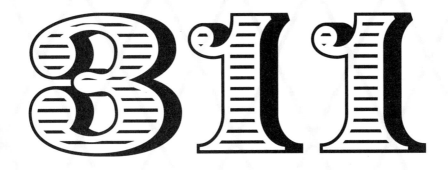

311

Give them another reason why Obama has GOT to go.

· ·

NO. 14.

He doesn't understand his people. To any liberal dumb enough to be mystified by Obama's consistently dismal approval ratings, just look at the way the president always puts socialistic principles before the needs of the American people. His administration's legal war against Arizona's attempt to enforce immigration law is a case in point. The United States has a serious illegal immigrant problem. So what does Obama do when the state of Arizona makes the intelligent— and nationally popular—decision to allow its police to question people about their

CONTINUED ON NEXT PAGE

CONTINUED FROM PREVIOUS PAGE

immigration status during routine stops? Why, he seeks to have the state law overturned in the courts, so as to pander to the hurt feelings of the Mexican government (which supplies the illegals) and to his hard-left sympathizers (who see the illegal immigrants as a future left-wing voting bloc). The American people will not forgive him for jeopardizing their security in this way.

312

Patiently explain to a liberal why their hero Michael Moore's *Capitalism: A Love Story* depends on an entirely false premise—that capitalism is the same as corporatism.

Most of Moore's targets in the movie are the unwieldy, corrupt corporations that his hero Obama has spent so much taxpayer money bribing and bailing out. They've got about as much to do with the free markets that conservatives favor as Michael Moore has with charm, wit, or healthy salads. And if he really has

CONTINUED ON NEXT PAGE

CONTINUED FROM PREVIOUS PAGE

such a problem with capitalism, what was he doing allowing movie theaters to charge audiences eight bucks a ticket? Shouldn't he have used some of the vast fortune he has earned from books and movies railing against capitalism so that his vital public service announcement could be put out for free?

313

Pick a fight with a liberal on:

SELF-ESTEEM.

One of the great excuses made for the poorer performances by certain ethnic groups is their "lack of self-esteem"—which comes, of course, from the sense of inferiority imposed on them either consciously or unconsciously by the white, elitist, capitalist, male hegemony. Much of this stems from research conducted by black socialist Kenneth B. Clark using his infamous "doll" tests. He showed black children in segregated schools a black doll and a white doll and asked which they preferred. When a majority chose the white doll, he argued that segregated schooling lowered black self-esteem. But Clark was a

CONTINUED ON NEXT PAGE

CONTINUED FROM PREVIOUS PAGE

professional grievance-monger and a fraud. What he did not mention was that in research he had conducted in integrated schools, black children were shown to be *even more likely* to choose the white doll over the black doll. Clark's junk sociology was the basis for sweeping legislation forcing integration in schools through wildly unpopular school busing programs that tore communities apart; and it's also responsible for more recent findings that American kids do worse than many of their international counterparts on academic tests—but think of themselves as being great, and much smarter than they really are. What self-esteem really is, is another liberal assault on a Christian virtue: namely, humility. We could all use a lot more of that.

314

Pick a fight with a liberal on:

LIBERAL MEDIA BIAS.

Quote the "great"—and remember to use the air quotes—Walter Cronkite: "I think most newspaper men by definition have to be liberal; if they're not liberal, by my definition of it, they can hardly be good newspapermen."

Quote the wisdom
of Al "Buzz" Gore:

"Welcome to President Clinton, Mrs. Clinton, and my fellow astronauts...."

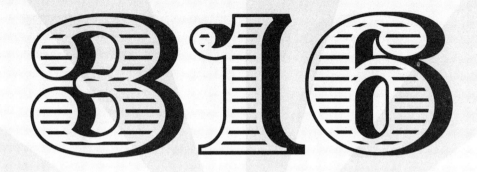

316

Tell a joke:

Q. Why should liberals be buried 100 feet below the ground?

A. Because deep down they are really good people.

317

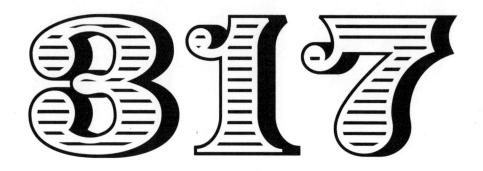

Start a rumor:

White House cutbacks have forced "Counter-terrorism Czar" John Brennan to supplement his meager income by taking on a weekend job as area local branch manager for al Qaeda (Washington, D.C., chapter). Though he tries his best to avoid any conflict of interest, sometimes the poor guy just can't help himself. Like when he "accidentally" had underwear bomber Farouk Abdulmutallab read his Miranda rights just an hour into questioning; when he made a speech claiming that "Jihad" is a "legitimate tenet of Islam" which means—ahem, nudge, nudge, wink, wink—an "inner struggle for purity"; when he referred to Jerusalem before a Muslim audience as "al Quds," thus legitimizing the (false) assertion that Islam has an originalist claim to the city.

318

Quote Competitive Enterprise Institute Founder Fred Smith Jr.

· ·

"The threat posed by humans to the natural environment is nothing compared to the threat to humans posed by global environmental policy."

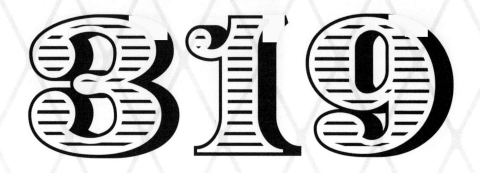

319

Settle down your liberal friends for a festive game that will provide hours of fun.

Give each of them a copy of the Obama administration's 86-page report (produced by Clinton-era appointees Togo West and Admiral Vernon Clark) on the Fort Hood massacre committed by an Islamist terrorist and see who can be the first to find a reference to Islam.

Here's the "funny" part: there isn't one.

320

Reclaim rock for conservatism:

Speculate that the Rolling Stones' "You Can't Always Get What You Want" was almost certainly an attempt by London School of Economics-educated Mick Jagger to convey to his youthful audience two of the bedrock concepts of conservatism: life is unfair; don't expect the state to bail you out.

321

Pick a fight with a liberal on:

"PEACE ACTIVISTS."

Oh, yeah right, like the "peace activists" on the "peace convoy" bringing aid to the people of Gaza in May 2010? The ones who engaged in the traditional "peace activist" activity before they set sail from Turkey of preparing suicide videos; the ones who armed themselves with iron bars, knives, and guns, and tried to beat up, slice open, and shoot the brutal Israeli soldiers who boarded their ships armed with paintball guns. So what you're saying, right, is that "peace" is the new "war"?

Find a feminist and see
if she has a sense of humor:

Q: How many men does it take to fix a woman's watch?

A: What does she need a watch for? There's a clock on the oven!

323

Give them another reason why Obama has GOT to go.

NO. 15.

He broke his promise to close the detention center at Guantanamo. Not that we *mind* exactly. We'd rather Gitmo stayed open for as long as the War on Terror lasts, which, the way Obama is handling things, looks like it might be forever. Obviously it makes sense to keep jihadists who are fanatically committed to the destruction of the West safely cooped up in their orange jumpsuits rather than trying to kill us all when we take a plane. But that's the point: it's so obvious we need Gitmo open that the fact that Obama promised otherwise on the campaign trail (Guantanamo to close by January 2010, he said) means he's either terminally naïve or a despicable liar. Neither handicap makes him suitable to be our president.

Conservative history:

Quote "liberal fascist" Woodrow Wilson as an early example of America-hating, One World Government addiction. Asked whether the League of Nations might compromise American sovereignty, he replied that he looked forward to the day "when men would be just as eager partisans of the sovereignty of mankind as they were now of their own national sovereignty."

Defend Israel.

Show them pictures of Gaza's ritzy new shopping mall; quote the Japanese journalist who said: "Gaza and the West Bank are the only places in the world where
I see refugees drive Mercedes"; remind them that life expectancy for Gaza Arabs—
seventy-two years—is nearly five years higher than the world average, with a
higher literacy rate than Turkey's. Then explain: "And it's ALL the result of years
and years of EVIL ISRAELI OPPRESSION!"

326

Pick a fight with a liberal on:

PEAK OIL.

"Peak oil"—the idea that we've reached the peak of oil production and that it's about to run out—is an S & M fantasy scenario designed by liberals to justify their fetish for higher taxation, greater government control, more regulation, and the mass switchover to expensive, pointless energy sources that don't work, such as wind and solar power. As Dennis Miller says: "Relax. We'll replace oil when we need to. American ingenuity will kick in and the next great fortune will be made. It's not pretty but it is historically accurate. We need to run out of oil first. That's why I drive an SUV—so we run out of it more quickly. I consider myself to be at the vanguard of the environmental movement and I think individuals who insist on driving hybrids are just prolonging our dilemma and I think that's just selfish...."

When the holidays roll around, always say:

"Merry Christmas," never "Happy Holidays." Not only do 70 percent of Americans prefer it—according to Rasmussen polls—but you are much more likely to offend a liberal. While 88 percent of Republican voters prefer "Merry Christmas," only 57 percent of Democrats do.

Single out all the liberal atheists in your neighborhood

for *ordeal by carol-singing.*

329

Quote Richard Lamm, former Democratic Governor of Colorado:

"Christmas is a time when kids tell Santa what they want and adults pay for it. Deficits are when adults tell the government what they want and their kids pay for it."

330

Sympathize with liberals who feel uncomfortable about celebrating "Christmas."

Helpfully suggest that they might want to celebrate the pagan festival of *Julfest* instead—where you still get to have a decorated tree in the house, but without those awkward Christian connotations. "After all," add, "it's what all the most dedicated Nazis used to do in Hitler's Germany, and they were pagan socialists just like you are…"

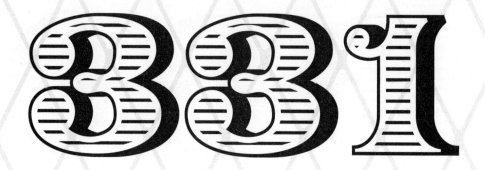

331

When talking about "Kwanzaa," put on a silly, fake-African voice, make inverted-commas signs with your fingers, and, if feeling energetic, perform a comedy, witchdoctor dance.

Explain that you are simply being true to the festival's long, rich, imaginative cultural heritage... invented in 1967 by a black activist Maulana Karenga (née Ronald McKinley Everett), who was subsequently imprisoned for felony assault and false imprisonment.

332

Make a point of dressing well and going to church on Sunday.

Wave to your sleepy-eyed, flip-flop-wearing slob of an atheistic neighbor and shout out, "We'll pray for you!"

Have children.

Liberals are too selfish and fussy to think of kids as anything but a bother or an expensive accoutrement to their lifestyle.

Mow your lawn

(a riding tractor mower is fine; so is a push mower for traditionalist conservatives) while smoking a pipe and wearing lace-up oxfords, a button down shirt (you can roll up the sleeves if it's hot), khaki pants, and a regimental tie, and say, "Nice day for a spin around the yard!"

335

While talking with your liberal friend, suddenly start sniffing the air, then brighten as if the light bulb has just gone off:

. . . .

"Oh, reliving the old hippie days, were you? It's okay to shower, you know; water's a renewable resource; it comes from rain...."

336

Force them to sit down and watch the movie *Patton*.

Then ask them just how well we'd have done in World War II with an army led by men like Barack ("We could learn from the Nazis' outreach to Islam") Obama, draft-dodging Bill Clinton, Al ("All these explosions must be bad for the environment") Gore, Jimmy ("America has to get over her inordinate fear of National Socialism") Carter....

Remind a liberal that California used to be a reliable Republican state.

It voted Republican in every presidential election from 1952 to 1992 with only one exception (1964). Remind a liberal further that in those days, California was renowned for having some of the most right-wing voting districts in the country (in Southern California's Orange County); and remind the liberal even further that in those days California was equally renowned for its prosperity. Since 1992, the state has been overwhelmingly Democrat, and—while flooded with illegal immigrants—native Californians have been fleeing to other states, and the economy has gone down the toilet. Is that all just a coincidence?

338

Show them the neglected conservative flick *The Wild Geese* with Roger Moore, Richard Burton, and Richard Harris.

A collection of truly free-market soldiers (mercenaries) blow the hell out of Communist, Cuban-aided Africans, to rescue a democratic African leader. True, the bad guy is a wealthy investor, as your liberal friend will undoubtedly point out to you, but you can say, "Yeah, you're right; he reminds me of George Soros."

339

Even an agnostic liberal might be a little taken aback to learn that *Rules for Radicals* by Saul Alinsky,

a book that inspired the likes of Barack Obama and Hillary Clinton, is dedicated to "the first radical known to man who rebelled against the establishment and did it so effectively that he at least won his own kingdom—Lucifer." Point out that Alinsky was at least one radical who knew where liberalism led.

Give a gift

Celebrate the "13 Days of Glory" that mark the siege of the Alamo (February 23 to March 6) by bringing your liberal friend a gift basket of thirteen John Wayne westerns, including, of course, *The Alamo*.

341

Invite your favorite liberal couple over for dinner.

Be sure to pull the seat out and then slide it in for the lady—and then do the same for the man. It's easy and so much fun to unman a liberal—and what's he going to do: complain that you're *not* being sexist?

342

Take up hunting (if you don't hunt already) and leave your kill in the back of your pickup truck.

Invite your liberal friend over and ask him if he'd like a cut of truly organic protein.

Liberal myth-busting:

If a liberal ever tries to justify government intrusion using the *argumentum reductio ad slaveram*—that, after all, it took federal government action (the Emancipation Proclamation) to free the slaves—remind him of what he never learned in school: the Emancipation Proclamation didn't free a single slave; it had no legal standing; and it didn't even extend to areas under Union control. It was a neat, diplomatic-rhetorical dodge to prevent foreign powers from recognizing the South (as it was no longer a war over Southern independence, which was diplomatically justifiable, but presumably a war over slavery, which was not). What ended slavery was two things liberals don't often like—the United States Army and a strict construction of the Constitution, enacting change through an approved constitutional amendment—not through judicial fiat or Obamaland czars or executive orders without true legal standing.

344

Give them another reason why Obama has GOT to go.

. . . .

NO. 16.

According to NASA administrator Charles Bolden, Obama now thinks it is more appropriate for America's space program to tout the alleged scientific contributions of Islam than it is to push the frontiers of space exploration. Forget about exploring Mars, the purpose of NASA is to raise Muslim self-esteem. Or, as Obama might put it: "Ask not what NASA can do for America's space program, ask what it can do for Islam!"

345

Keep a life-size cardboard cutout of Pamela Anderson from her *Baywatch* days and stand it next to a life-size cardboard cutout of Joe Biden.

. . . .

When your liberal friend asks you, "What's up with this?" tell him you keep them to remind you of the difference between a real boob and a fake one.

Reclaim Rock for conservatism:

Beneath the American flag, and the "Don't Tread on Me" flag you fly in your front yard, fly an Elvis Presley rebel flag (available from an online outlet near you—the best ones have "the King" in a cowboy hat).

347

Reclaim Rock for conservatism (or in this case, country-rock):

Invite your liberal friend over for a barbecue serenaded with anti-pc hits from Hank Williams Jr. like "A Country Boy Can Survive" and "If the South Woulda Won."

You're Invited!

348

Country Music is almost by definition offensive to liberals,

but just to make sure it stays that way, as part of your "13 Days of Glory" Alamo celebration host a Tex-Mex dinner featuring all the best conservative country songs, from Merle Haggard's "I'm Just an Okie from Muskogee" to Toby Keith's "Angry American." If your liberal friend scowls, asks him to explain why he can't, in his multicultural way, appreciate an authentic American musical art form and show some understanding for people different from himself—you know, people who love America, aren't ashamed of flying the flag, are proud of our military, enjoy having a good time....

349

Have your high school son invite his friends to come over in swim shorts and bikinis for a car wash fundraiser, "Babes and Buds against Burqas."

Have another to raise money to build a church in Mecca.

You're Invited

350

Practice fly-casting on your front lawn.

When your liberal friend comes over and asks the inevitable, "Oh, so you're a fly-fisherman (or fisherperson)," shrug your shoulders and say, "Not really, I just do this in the yard to relax. When I go fishing I've found dynamite gets you a lot more bang for your buck."

Say grace before meals.

Bringing God into the picture always puts liberals ill at ease, because it reminds them you think there's a power more important than government.

352

Make sure your wife has a ready supply of conservative novels to recommend to her ladies book club.

· ·

A few good starters: *Brideshead Revisited* by Evelyn Waugh; *Sense and Sensibility* by Jane Austen; *The Old Limey* by H. W. Crocker III; *A Confederacy of Dunces* by John Kennedy O'Toole.

Next time a liberal upbraids you

for "maintaining narrow, traditional moral values" remind him that "tradition" is simply the inherited wisdom of our ancestors, which keeps us from making moral fools of ourselves, and anyway, which of these traditional moral values would he flat-out like to do away with: compassion, fidelity, honesty, restraint, deference, courage, chivalry, self-denial....(Actually, all of them, but he won't be able to say that.)

Start a "Take a Liberal to Lunch" program

to provide counseling for liberals whose high hopes for hope 'n' change are running out.

355

On Easter day, as you're driving to church, call out to your slobovian, atheistic, liberal neighbor sitting on his porch:

. . . .

"Happy Easter! Our Savior liveth! Sorry yours won't get reelected!"

356

On November 10, celebrate the birthday of the Marine Corps.

If you're within driving distance of the Marine Corps Museum (in Quantico, Virginia) take your liberal friend there. Marvel innocently at the lack of Obama bumper stickers in the parking lot.

357

Give them a copy of Ayn Rand's *Atlas Shrugged.*

The novel's come-on of violent sex, atheistic individualism, and vaguely fascistic yearnings might make it attractive to your average liberal and help to win him over by stages to its better libertarian elements.

358

When your liberal neighbors knock excitedly on your door to show you ultrasound pictures of the baby they're expecting,

. . . .

look mortified and then say, "But surely, it's not yet a child, it's still a choice."

359

Ask your liberal neighbor to explain the logic of Obama's "stimulus" pork program.

Say, "So let me get this right, the government takes money from taxpayers to put more workers on the government payroll that is paid for by taxpayers, and this helps the economy how exactly?" When he goes on to give a vague (and probably inaccurate) Keynesian explanation, you can cut him off with, "By that explanation, thieves are good for the economy, too—they help spread the wealth around; but I'll stick with the old-fashioned idea that we don't need the government to spread the wealth around, we can do that ourselves with our own free-market choices that support real free-market jobs and independent charities. What's the beef you liberals have with freedom anyway?"

360

Ask a liberal:

Q: What's the difference between a Democratic Congress and a drunken sailor?

A: More than a trillion dollars.

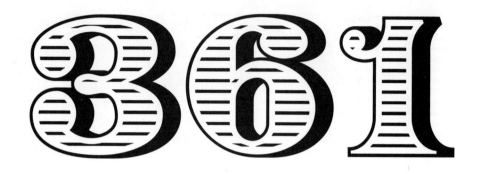

361

Confide in a liberal that if you had your way, the federal government would abolish the Department of Homeland Security (another big government boondoggle) and the Department of Defense.

When your liberal friend expresses his surprise, say, "Yeah, I think we should streamline that whole kit-and-caboodle to make it what it used to be: the Department of War."

Quote Teddy Roosevelt:

"A gentleman told me recently that he doubted I would vote for the Angel Gabriel if found at the head of the Democratic Party, to which I responded that the Angel Gabriel would never be found in such company. Speaking quite dispassionately, and simply as a historian, the Democrats can be trusted invariably to walk in the darkness even when to walk in the light would be manifestly to their advantage."

363

On Pearl Harbor Day (December 7th, I hope I don't have to remind you), tell your liberal neighbor that the answer to Islamist terror is the same as it was to defeating crazy-eyed Japanese militarism.

"You don't mean..." and before he can get the words out, just say, "Uh-huh," and keep him guessing.

364

Give your small children toy guns,

· ·

and tell your liberal friend, "Yeah, I think this is the best way to break them in so they can handle the real thing when they're six or seven."

365

Most annoying of all for any liberal

. . . .

would be for you to have door-stopped him with 364 of these ideas, and now…
ha-ha-ha, we start them all over again!

Holidays,
Birthdays,
and Anniversaries

January

1

Why not make it your New Year's resolution to use this book to annoy liberals? Start on New Year's Day.

Invite all your liberal friends over to share your joy: after this year, there'll only be ONE more full year of Obama; and this time in two years he'll be just weeks away from retiring to Kenya, Saudi Arabia, North Korea, or wherever in the world they're still prepared to give the guy asylum after all the mess he's made.

January

17

On his birthday, quote Benjamin Franklin:

. . . .

"They that can give up essential liberty to obtain a little temporary safety, deserve neither liberty nor safety." Tell your liberal friend Franklin was referring to government-controlled health care.

January

On Martin Luther King Day

ask why we have a public holiday named after a Vietcong-supporting radical who—in a 1967 speech—compared U.S. forces in Vietnam to Nazis. (True, by the way.) That ought to pull your liberal friend up short. If he recovers his wits and says MLK was right about Vietnam, tell him to talk to some Boat People. In the meantime, you'll celebrate Lee-Jackson Day, because Robert E. Lee and Stonewall Jackson were officers and gentlemen.

February

When Black History Month (formerly known as February) begins,

always refer to it as Fake History Month. Then explain that you refuse to support a racist event which essentially demeans African Americans by subtly implying that they are too bigoted and dumb to relate to any historical event which doesn't involve people with the right skin tone.

February

On Ronald Reagan's birthday, quote him:

. . . .

"The nine most terrifying words in the English language are: 'I'm from the government and I'm here to help.'"

February

Use Joseph Schumpeter's birthday as an excuse to explain exactly what was wrong with Obama's "Porkulus" package.

Using taxpayers' money to prop up failing industries that the market no longer deems viable is a classic socialist error: what a healthy economy really needs is Schumpeter's "creative destruction," whereby the death of an old industry creates space for the birth of a new industry which in turn generates more money and more jobs. Explain that the reasons socialists like Obama hate this process are a) they can't control it, and b) it works.

February

9

On his birthday, quote Thomas Paine, who foresaw 250 years ago just where the United States could go wrong:

"Government, even in its best state, is but a necessary evil; in its worst state, an intolerable one."

February

22

On his birthday, quote George Washington as a reminder that from first to last, all of America's greatest presidents have believed above all in liberty:

"Government is not reason; it is not eloquence; it is force. Like fire, it is a dangerous servant and a fearful master."

April Fool's Day

Comment to your liberal friends:

"Barack Obama, Al Gore—Nobel Prize Winners! Ha, ha, ha! Oh those Norwegians—they do light up the world with their practical jokes, don't they? Ha, ha, ha, ha!"

Easter

On Easter day, as you're driving to church, call out to your slobovian, atheistic, liberal neighbor sitting on his porch:

. . . .

"Happy Easter! Our Savior liveth! Sorry yours won't get reelected!"

April

20

On Adolf Hitler's birthday, call up all your liberal friends to congratulate them.

When they express outrage, respond with deep surprise: "But I thought...well, I thought Hitler was kind of a role model for you socialists? He loved big government...and furry animals...and hated smoking...and thought we needed to get beyond restrictive Judeo-Christian morality...and was pro-Muslim..."

April

22

Celebrate Earth Day

. . . .

by reminding liberals of all the whacko predictions made by environmentalists in 1970, the year the event was founded: a new Ice Age (*Newsweek*); a world "eleven degrees colder by the year 2000" (Kenneth Watt); by 1985 air pollution to reduce the amount of sunlight reaching earth by one half (*Life* magazine); by 1995 between 75 and 85 percent of all species to be extinct (Earth Day founder Gaylord Nelson); mass starvation (Earth Day organizer Denis Hayes). Say: "Thank you, thank you, Earth Day! If those 20 million hippies hadn't taken the day off work, we'd all be dead by now!"

April
30

Just as you called your liberal friends on Adolf Hitler's birthday,

annoy the heck out of them by doing it again on the anniversary of Hitler's death and offer your profound condolences.

When they get cross, tell them you feel their pain. As a conservative, you know how hard it is to be persecuted for holding views some find unfashionable. Say you won't condemn them for being socialist fellow travelers of Herr Hitler and that their secret is safe, just so long as they agree not to try any of that Sieg Heil stuff when your kids are anywhere nearby.

May

8

Pick a fight with a liberal on Friedrich Hayek's birthday.

Quote him: "The basis of [the classical liberal] argument is that nobody can know who knows best and that the only way by which we can find out is through a social process in which everybody is allowed to try and see what he can do." Exactly! This shows up the rottenness at the core of all liberal arguments: built into them is the assumption that liberals know what is best for us. But they don't. If they did, how do you explain the fact that we're now being run by the Obama administration?

June

Quote the great free-marketeer Claude Frederic Bastiat on his birthday:

· ·

"Each of us has a natural right, from God, to defend his person, his liberty and his property."

July

On Independence Day, quote Calvin Coolidge (whose birthday it is) to show the essential difference between a good and bad president:

"It is much more important to kill bad bills than to pass good ones."

August

6

Time to invite your liberal friends 'round for another barbecue.

Why? To celebrate the day when the lives of hundreds of thousands of young American and Allied servicemen were saved thanks to President Truman's fine, principled decision to drop the atom bomb on Hiroshima. Serve Kamikaze cocktails (natch): equal parts Vodka, Triple Sec, and lime juice.

You're Invited!

August

Call your liberal friends to ask why they haven't yet thanked you for your Hiroshima Day celebration barbecue and Kamikaze cocktails.

Was it something you said? Tell them if they like, they can come over for another celebration tonight because it's Nagasaki Day (August 9), anniversary of the second atom bomb which finally led to the surrender of evil, warmongering Imperial Japan. Quote literary historian Paul Fussell on how it felt to hear the news: "We learned to our astonishment that we would not be obliged in a few months

CONTINUED ON NEXT PAGE

CONTINUED FROM PREVIOUS PAGE

to rush up the beaches near Tokyo assault-firing while being machine-gunned, mortared, and shelled, and for all the practiced phlegm of our tough facades we broke down and cried with relief and joy. We were going to live."

August

17

On this day in 1945, George Orwell's *Animal Farm* was published.

It's so easy to read, even liberals can understand it. Donate two dozen or so copies to your kids' class. Make sure to underline the passage where Orwell encapsulates the hypocrisy of the liberal notion of social justice: "All animals are equal. But some animals are more equal than others."

Columbus Day

On Columbus Day, loudly express your gratitude that America was taken away from backward, cruel, and bloodthirsty Indian tribes and given over to Christian European civilization.

Go further and tell your liberal friends that you've always admired how Cortez and his small band of men conquered the Aztec empire, abolishing a culture based on human sacrifice. As they stand there spluttering, you can rub it in: "You have a problem with that?"

October

30

Quote John Adams on his birthday:

. . . .

"All good government is and must be republican." Or, if you prefer, with special application to the Obama administration and the current Supreme Court: "The jaws of power are always open to devour, and her arm is always stretched out, if possible, to destroy the freedom of thinking, speaking, and writing."

Halloween

Help your kids to make Carol Browner and Al Gore horror masks—

. . . .

on unbleached, recycled, Fair Trade paper, obviously—then encourage them to go 'round bugging the hell out of your liberal neighbors shaking a begging bowl and yelling: "Cap 'n' trade! Cap 'n' trade!"

November
10

On November 10, celebrate the birthday of the Marine Corps.

If you're within driving distance of the Marine Corps Museum (in Quantico, Virginia) take your liberal friend there. Marvel innocently at the lack of Obama bumper stickers in the parking lot.

Thanksgiving

Give thanks that you've won life's lottery:

. . . .

You're an American and you're a conservative; you are one righteous dude!

December

**On Pearl Harbor Day,
tell your liberal neighbor that
the answer to Islamist terror
is the same as it was to defeating
crazy-eyed Japanese-militarism.**

. . . .

"You don't mean …" and before he can get the words out, just say, "Uh-huh,"
and keep him guessing.

Christmas

No. 1. When the holidays roll around, always say: "Merry Christmas," never "Happy Holidays." Not only do 70 percent of Americans prefer it—according to Rasmussen polls—but you are much more likely to offend a liberal. While 88 percent of Republican voters prefer "Merry Christmas," only 57 percent of Democrats do.

No. 2. Single out all the liberal atheists in your neighborhood for *ordeal by carol-singing.*

No. 3. Quote Richard Lamm, former Democratic Governor of Colorado: "Christmas is a time when kids tell Santa what they want and adults pay for it. Deficits are when adults tell the government what they want and their kids pay for it."

CONTINUED ON NEXT PAGE

No. 4. Sympathize with liberals who feel uncomfortable about celebrating "Christmas." Helpfully suggest that they might want to celebrate the pagan festival of *Julfest* instead—where you still get to have a decorated tree in the house, but without those awkward Christian connotations. "After all," add, "it's what all the most dedicated Nazis used to do in Hitler's Germany, and they were pagan socialists just like you are…"

No. 5. When talking about "Kwanzaa" put on a silly, fake-African voice, make inverted-commas signs with your fingers, and, if feeling energetic, perform a comedy, witchdoctor dance. Explain that you are simply being true to the festival's long, rich, imaginative cultural heritage…invented in 1967 by a black activist Maulana Karenga (née Ronald McKinley Everett), who was subsequently imprisoned for felony assault and false imprisonment.